> "Sacrifices during Lent are a response to the salvation we have received through Christ."

Study Suggestions 6
How to Study the Bible 8
The Attributes of God 10
Timeline of Scripture 12
Metanarrative of Scripture 14
How to Use This Study 16

PART I: THE REALITY OF OUR SIN + THE ONE WHO FORGIVES OUR SIN

Day One:
Understanding Our Sin Problem 20

Day Two:
Experiencing a World
Created and Tainted 25

Day Three:
Recognizing Our Sin
and Need for the Savior 30

Day Four:
Walking in Repentance 35

Rest Reflection 40

Day Five:
Taking Up Our Cross 42

Day Six:
Seeking the Kingdom 47

Day Seven:
Putting Off and Putting On 52

Day Eight:
Living Sacrifices 57

Day Nine:
Pursuing Holiness 62

Day Ten:
Walking by the Spirit 67

Rest Reflection 72

PART II: THE SINS WE WRESTLE WITH

Day Eleven:
Considering Our Sin 76

Day Twelve:
Moving from Unbelief to Belief 79

Day Thirteen:
Worshiping God over
Everything Else 84

Day Fourteen:
Trading Apathy for Mercy 89

Day Fifteen:
Turning Hatred into Love 94

Day Sixteen:
Forgoing Greed for
True Satisfaction 99

Rest Reflection 104

Day Seventeen:
Forsaking Discontentment
and Finding Contentment 106

Day Eighteen:
Fighting Lust with
Christ's Power 111

Day Nineteen:
Going from Hopelessness
to Hopefulness 116

Day Twenty:
Trading Harshness
for Gentleness 121

IN THIS STUDY

Day Twenty-One:
Choosing Graciousness
over Gossip 126

Day Twenty-Two:
Putting Humility
in the Place of Pride 131

Rest Reflection 136

Day Twenty-Three:
Trading Selfishness for Selflessness 138

Day Twenty-Four:
Seeking Unity over Division 143

Day Twenty-Five:
Embracing Honesty over Hypocrisy 148

Day Twenty-Six:
Pursuing Patience over
Prideful Impatience 153

Day Twenty-Seven:
Extending Forgiveness
Instead of Unforgiveness 158

Day Twenty-Eight:
Replacing Sinful Anger
with Christ's Righteousness 163

Rest Reflection 168

Day Twenty-Nine:
Being Kind Instead
of Judgmental 170

Day Thirty:
Fighting Bitterness with
God's Faithfulness 175

Day Thirty-One:
Resisting Jealousy by
Resting in Christ 180

Day Thirty-Two:
Choosing Gratitude
over Grumbling 185

Day Thirty-Three:
Loving Truth over Lies 190

Day Thirty-Four:
Speaking Graciously
Instead of Obscenely 195

Rest Reflection 200

PART III: HOPE FOR OUR SIN

Day Thirty-Five:
Living Out Our Freedom 204

Day Thirty-Six:
Remembering Christ's Forgiveness 207

Day Thirty-Seven:
Dwelling on Christ's Sympathy 212

Day Thirty-Eight:
Resting in God's Power 217

Day Thirty-Nine:
Celebrating Christ's Victory 222

Day Forty:
Looking toward
the Hope of Heaven 227

Rest Reflection 232

What is the Gospel? 236

Bibliography 238

Study Suggestions

We believe that the Bible is true, trustworthy, and timeless and that it is vitally important for all believers. These study suggestions are intended to help you more effectively study Scripture as you seek to know and love God through His Word.

SUGGESTED STUDY TOOLS

- ☐ Bible

- ☐ Double-spaced, printed copy of the Scripture passages that this study covers (You can use a website like www.biblegateway.com to copy the text of a passage and print out a double-spaced copy to be able to mark on easily.)

- ☐ Journal to write notes or prayers

- ☐ Pens, colored pencils, and highlighters

- ☐ Dictionary to look up unfamiliar words

HOW TO USE THIS STUDY

 Pray

Begin your study time in prayer. Ask God to reveal Himself to you, help you understand what you are reading, and transform you with His Word (Psalm 119:18).

 Read Scripture

Before you read what is written in each day of the study itself, read the assigned passages of Scripture for that day. Use your double-spaced copy to circle, underline, highlight, draw arrows, and mark in any way you would like to help you dig deeper as you work through a passage.

 Read Study Content

Read the daily written content provided for the current study day.

 Respond

Answer the questions that appear at the end of each study day.

How to Study the Bible

The inductive method provides tools for deeper and more intentional Bible study. To study the Bible inductively, work through the steps below after reading background information on the book.

01 Observation & Comprehension
KEY QUESTION: WHAT DOES THE TEXT SAY?

After reading the daily Scripture in its entirety at least once, begin working with smaller portions of the Scripture. Read a passage of Scripture repetitively, and then mark the following items in the text:

- Key or repeated words and ideas
- Key themes
- Transition words (e.g., therefore, but, because, if/then, likewise, etc.)
- Lists
- Comparisons and contrasts
- Commands
- Unfamiliar words (look these up in a dictionary)
- Questions you have about the text

02 Interpretation
KEY QUESTION: WHAT DOES THE TEXT MEAN?

Once you have annotated the text, work through the following steps to help you interpret its meaning:

- Read the passage in other versions for a better understanding of the text.
- Read cross-references to help interpret Scripture with Scripture.
- Paraphrase or summarize the passage to check for understanding.
- Identify how the text reflects the metanarrative of Scripture, which is the story of creation, fall, redemption, and restoration.
- Read trustworthy commentaries if you need further insight into the meaning of the passage.

Application
KEY QUESTION: HOW SHOULD THE TRUTH OF THIS PASSAGE CHANGE ME?

Bible study is not merely an intellectual pursuit. The truths about God, ourselves, and the gospel that we discover in Scripture should produce transformation in our hearts and lives. Answer the following questions and prompts as you consider what you have learned in your study:

- What attributes of God's character are revealed in the passage?
- Consider places where the text directly states the character of God, as well as how His character is revealed through His words and actions.
- What do I learn about myself in light of who God is?
- Consider how you fall short of God's character, how the text reveals your sin nature, and what it says about your new identity in Christ.
- How should this truth change me?
- A passage of Scripture may contain direct commands telling us what to do or warnings about sins to avoid in order to help us grow in holiness. Other times, our application flows out of seeing ourselves in light of God's character. As we pray and reflect on how God is calling us to change in light of His Word, we should be asking questions like, "How should I pray for God to change my heart?" and "What practical steps can I take toward cultivating habits of holiness?"

The Attributes of God

Eternal
God has no beginning and no end. He always was, always is, and always will be.
HAB. 1:12 / REV. 1:8 / ISA. 41:4

Faithful
God is incapable of anything but fidelity. He is loyally devoted to His plan and purpose.
2 TIM. 2:13 / DEUT. 7:9 / HEB. 10:23

Good
God is pure; there is no defilement in Him. He is unable to sin, and all He does is good.
GEN. 1:31 / PS. 34:8 / PS. 107:1

Gracious
God is kind, giving us gifts and benefits we do not deserve.
2 KINGS 13:23 / PS. 145:8
ISA. 30:18

Holy
God is undefiled and unable to be in the presence of defilement. He is sacred and set-apart.
REV. 4:8 / LEV. 19:2 / HAB. 1:13

Incomprehensible
God is high above and beyond human understanding. He is unable to be fully known.
PS. 145:3 / ISA. 55:8-9
ROM. 11:33-36

Immutable
God does not change. He is the same yesterday, today, and tomorrow.
1 SAM. 15:29 / ROM. 11:29
JAMES 1:17

Infinite
God is limitless. He exhibits all of His attributes perfectly and boundlessly.
ROM. 11:33-36 / ISA. 40:28
PS. 147:5

Jealous
God is desirous of receiving the praise and affection He rightly deserves.
EXOD. 20:5 / DEUT. 4:23-24
JOSH. 24:19

Just
God governs in perfect justice. He acts in accordance with justice. In Him, there is no wrongdoing or dishonesty.
ISA. 61:8 / DEUT. 32:4 / PS. 146:7-9

Loving
God is eternally, enduringly, steadfastly loving and affectionate. He does not forsake or betray His covenant love.
JOHN 3:16 / EPH. 2:4-5 / 1 JOHN 4:16

Merciful
God is compassionate, withholding from us the wrath that we deserve.
TITUS 3:5 / PS. 25:10
LAM. 3:22-23

Omnipotent

God is all-powerful; His strength is unlimited.

MATT. 19:26 / JOB 42:1-2
JER. 32:27

Omnipresent

God is everywhere; His presence is near and permeating.

PROV. 15:3 / PS. 139:7-10
JER. 23:23-24

Omniscient

God is all-knowing; there is nothing unknown to Him.

PS. 147:4 / I JOHN 3:20
HEB. 4:13

Patient

God is long-suffering and enduring. He gives ample opportunity for people to turn toward Him.

ROM. 2:4 / 2 PET. 3:9 / PS. 86:15

Self-Existent

God was not created but exists by His power alone.

PS. 90:1-2 / JOHN 1:4 / JOHN 5:26

Self-Sufficient

God has no needs and depends on nothing, but everything depends on God.

ISA. 40:28-31 / ACTS 17:24-25
PHIL. 4:19

Sovereign

God governs over all things; He is in complete control.

COL. 1:17 / PS. 24:1-2
1 CHRON. 29:11-12

Truthful

God is our measurement of what is fact. By Him we are able to discern true and false.

JOHN 3:33 / ROM. 1:25 / JOHN 14:6

Wise

God is infinitely knowledgeable and is judicious with His knowledge.

ISA. 46:9-10 / ISA. 55:9 / PROV. 3:19

Wrathful

God stands in opposition to all that is evil. He enacts judgment according to His holiness, righteousness, and justice.

PS. 69:24 / JOHN 3:36 / ROM. 1:18

Timeline of Scripture

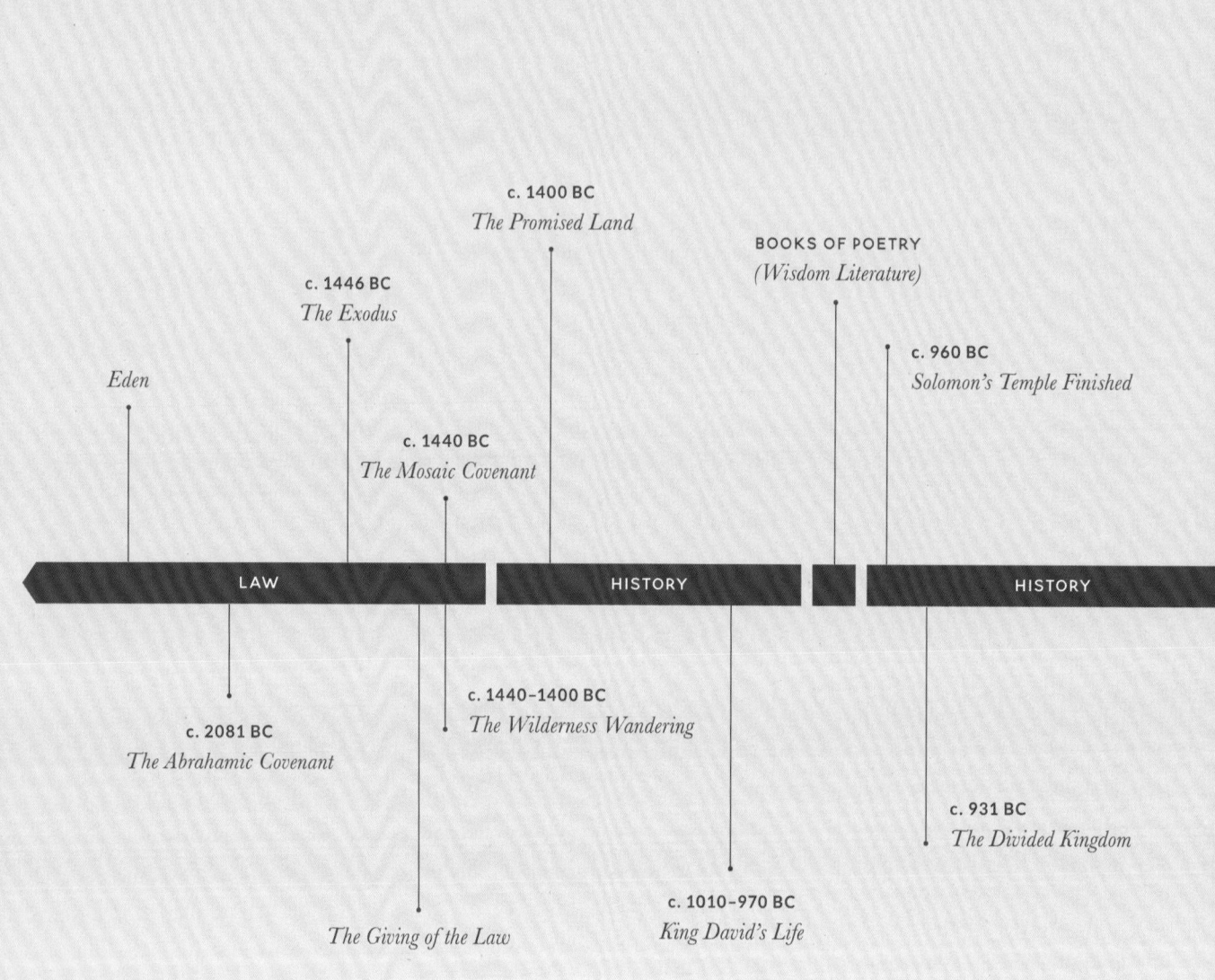

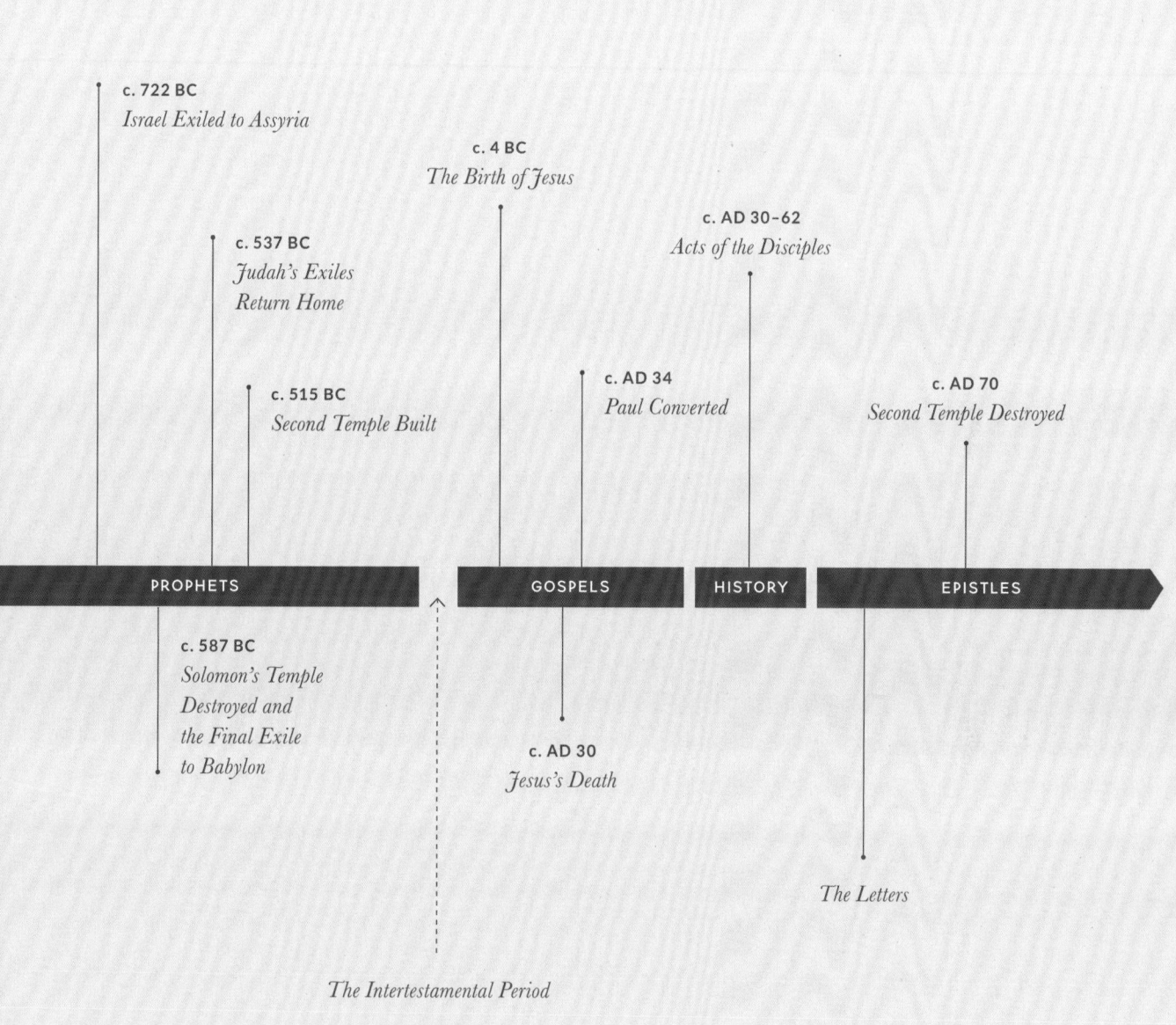

Timeline of Scripture

Metanarrative of Scripture

Creation

In the beginning, God created the universe. He made the world and everything in it. He created humans in His own image to be His representatives on the earth.

Fall

The first humans, Adam and Eve, disobeyed God by eating from the fruit of the Tree of Knowledge of Good and Evil. Their disobedience impacted the whole world. The punishment for sin is death, and because of Adam's original sin, all humans are sinful and condemned to death.

Redemption

God sent His Son to become a human and redeem His people. Jesus Christ lived a sinless life but died on the cross to pay the penalty for sin. He resurrected from the dead and ascended into heaven. All who put their faith in Jesus are saved from death and freely receive the gift of eternal life.

Restoration

One day, Jesus Christ will return again and restore all that sin destroyed. He will usher in a new heaven and new earth where all who trust in Him will live eternally with glorified bodies in the presence of God.

HOW TO USE THIS STUDY

Welcome to *From Death to Life: 40 Days of Dying to Self and Living for Christ*! As you embark on this forty-day study, it is our hope that you will be equipped to face the sin in your life as you learn and experience the freedom that comes from Christ alone.

Though this study may be used any time of the year, it was specifically designed to be used as a companion for the season of Lent, helping you prepare your heart for the joy of Easter. So, before we get into the specifics of this study, let us first take a closer look at what Lent is and how it has been observed over the years.

The History of Lent

The Church began observing the season of Lent as a way to help Christians intentionally prepare their hearts for the celebration of Easter. Lent is forty days long (excluding Sundays), and it begins on Ash Wednesday and concludes on Holy Saturday. Historically, it has been observed as a time for believers to be devoted to prayer and fasting.

How Lent Is Observed Today

Interestingly, the structure of Lent has varied through the years. In the past, the forty days of Lent involved prayer and fasting from a particular food. The idea behind this fasting is to reflect Jesus's forty days of fasting in the wilderness before beginning His ministry (Luke 4:1–13).

However, in our current day and age, what people choose to give up during Lent is their own choice: some may give up a type of food, while others may give up a tangible item or a form of technology. Either way, the choice to give something up reflects a believer's desire to make some sort of sacrifice. Like sacrificing food, we give up something that we often rely upon so that we can rely wholeheartedly on the Lord. When we feel pulled toward that thing we have given up, we are reminded to depend on the Lord above all things.

However, we must not see whatever sacrifice we make during Lent as the means to earn salvation with God. Rather, sacrifices during Lent are a response to the salvation we have received through Christ. As we sacrifice, we are reminded of the sacrifice Jesus made for our sake. Even if you do not choose to give something up, Lent is still a special time that points you to Jesus.

In addition to fasting during Lent, many people take time to reflect on their sins. Often, what someone chooses to give up during Lent is connected to a particular sinful habit they wish to remove or change. While it is not wrong to reflect on and seek to remove sin during Lent, it is possible to go about Lent with the incorrect posture. For example, some may view Lent as a time to temporarily keep themselves away from something "bad" until they can pick it back up again after Lent. In fact, this is why many people view the holiday Mardi Gras (which takes place the day before Lent begins) as a time to indulge in whatever they can before stopping for the forty days of Lent.

About This Study

We have written *From Death to Life* to help you cultivate a proper heart posture during the Lenten season and beyond. If you decide to follow the study during Lent, the first week of the study will allow you to begin on Ash Wednesday, while the last week of the study will enable you to finish with a hymn reflection on Easter Sunday.

This study is broken up into three parts. In Part 1, we will discuss the reality of our sin, our need for Jesus, and what it looks like to live for Christ. Part 2 will cover the sins we often struggle with as believers and how the gospel meets us in this struggle. And finally, Part 3 will discuss the hope we have in Christ as we fight against sin. It is our prayer that you will come to know and experience the freedom Christ offers you in a deeper and more meaningful way as you rely on the Holy Spirit to continually transform you, bringing you from death to life.

> Sacrifices during Lent are a response to the salvation we have received through Christ.

The Reality of Our Sin and the One Who Forgives Our Sin

DAY ONE

There is only one person who can
truly cure our sinful hearts,
and that person is Jesus Christ.

day one

UNDERSTANDING OUR SIN PROBLEM

Read Romans 6:1–11

Sin. No matter how much we try to ignore or push down the reality of sin, it is all around us. Sin plagues our society, manifesting itself in broken systems and marginalized people. Sin taints our workplaces, breeding love of power, excusing manipulation, and highlighting glory. Sin crawls into our homes and friendships, causing and perpetuating toxic relationships and fragmented families. But just as sin covers every inch of our world, so does it cover every inch of our hearts.

We may believe that we are good people, but our thoughts, words, and actions say otherwise. Even if we do and say what is right at times, sin bubbles up inside of us and spills out at some point. Jeremiah 17:9 tells us that our hearts are deceitful and incurable, and we see evidence of this truth when we sin, whether it be lashing out at a family member or passing judgment upon someone in our mind.

As humans, we try to cure our sinful hearts in our own power. But we cannot do anything on our own to cure our sinfulness. There is only one person who can truly cure our sinful hearts, and that person is Jesus Christ. Though we are desperately wicked and do not deserve forgiveness, Jesus cleanses our hearts with His grace. If we trust and believe in Him, Jesus washes away our sins and gives us new hearts that desire to obey and honor Him (Ezekiel 36:25–27).

But Jesus does not only give us new hearts—He gives us new lives. When we come to faith in Christ, our old sinful selves essentially "die," and we are given new selves. This is called regeneration, the process by which we are "born again." This new life causes our relationship with sin to change. Through Christ's grace and forgiveness, sin's grip on us is released, and we are no longer enslaved to sin. Our lives reflect the death and resurrection of our Savior as our sinful selves are put to death and our new, redeemed selves are made alive in Christ.

In the first part of this study, we will take a look at the reality of our sins and how Jesus forgives our sins. We will consider what makes our sin serious and our need for Christ's intervention. But we will also examine the new way of life Jesus calls us to. Through it all, we will see how the gospel is the answer to our sin problem. When we meditate on the gospel and center our lives around it, we cultivate our obedience to God and our dependence on Him. So may this part of the study challenge you to keep the gospel at the center of all you do and motivate you to further obey the One who brought you from death to life.

> Jesus does not only give us new hearts — He gives us new lives.

day one reflection

Write out a prayer below, asking God to prepare
your heart as you begin this study.

> The gospel is the answer to our sin problem.

DAY TWO

Sin brings death, but God brings life.

day two

EXPERIENCING A WORLD CREATED AND TAINTED

Read Genesis 1–3

People crying. Wars waging. Storms raging. Groups fighting. This is what we experience because of the sinful world in which we live. The sin and suffering we see and face point us to the reality that creation is broken. But it was not meant to be this way. Though this broken world is all we know, creation once lived with no spot of sin. In the beginning, God created a world that was filled with goodness.

Genesis 1–2 paints a picture of what our world used to be like. God spoke a world of beauty and abundance into existence, crafting it together with His intentional hands (Isaiah 48:13). He formed the clouds in the sky, the flowers of the field, the fish in the sea — and all of it was good. Even humans were created good and crafted in the likeness of God to reflect His holiness on the earth.

Can you imagine this world of pure goodness? We receive whispers of this goodness when we gaze upon a sunset that takes our breath away or witness a mother bird caring for her young, but situations of suffering and pain pull us back into reality. The world around us is not what we see in the opening pages of Scripture, but the fact that God called it "good" in the beginning reveals His original design for creation. Creation was never meant to be corrupt. It was meant to be a place of constant peace, harmony, and rest.

All that humanity had to do to maintain this peace, harmony, and rest was obey the Lord. In fact, they only had to obey one major command: to not eat from the Tree of the Knowledge of Good and Evil. As long as they kept this command, humanity could continue to enjoy the abundance around them and their intimate relationship with God. We know from the brokenness in our world and hearts that, sadly, this command was not kept. When Satan took the form of a serpent and tempted Eve, Eve listened to Satan's twisted words over the words of the Lord. She took and ate from the forbidden tree, and so did Adam. Within what was likely a matter of minutes, God's good creation changed.

Sin entered the world because of Adam and Eve's disobedience, and sin always results in consequences. Mankind now experiences hard work, pain, and bodies that will one day perish. But while it is not stated explicitly within Genesis, humanity also faces spiritual death. This is because sin deserves to be punished, and "the wages of sin is death" (Romans 6:23). Sin separates God and man and causes humanity to march toward an eternity of permanent separation from God. We see this separation in Genesis 3:23–24 as Adam and Eve were forced out of the garden, revealing that their perfect relationship with God was broken.

Genesis 3 records the brokenness and weighty consequences that sin creates. But nestled within these consequences is a promise of hope and deliverance. Genesis 3:15 reveals how from Adam and Eve's offspring would come someone who would crush Satan. This person would experience affliction themselves, but they would ultimately triumph over Satan. God's promise in Genesis 3:15 points to Jesus, who defeated sin and death through His death and resurrection. God's promise of salvation reveals how God is a God of grace. Though sin was brought into the world, God put forth a plan of redemption out of His abundant grace and love.

Genesis 1–3 teaches us that sin brings death, but God brings life. Pursuing our own desires, like Adam and Eve did, leads us away from the God of life and down a path of eternal death. Sin may promise to give us satisfaction, but it only steals, kills, and destroys (John 10:10). Therefore, if we want to do something about the sin that taints our hearts, we need to come to God. We need to come to the One who frees us from sin, forgives our disobedience, and saves us from death. And through Christ, we are able to come to God and receive this salvation and restoration. When we put our faith in Jesus, our relationship with God is restored, and we are rescued from spiritual death.

When we come to God through Christ, we not only receive salvation from our sins but hope in our sins. God not only promises to restore those who trust and believe in Christ, but He also promises to restore the entire world, bringing it to a place of perfection (Revelation 21). Therefore, we can trust the Lord and hope in Him as we continue to battle sin within ourselves and in the world. Though sin runs rampant, it cannot outrun God's power and promises.

> When we put our faith in Jesus, our relationship with God is restored, and we are rescued from spiritual death.

day two reflection

How does knowing that God created everything good
help us understand where sin came from?

What does it say about God's character that He not only created
everything good but also put forth a plan to remove sin?

How does God's promise to remove sin once and for all
give you hope as you struggle with sin?

> "A thief comes only to steal and kill and destroy. I have come so that they may have life and have it in abundance."
>
> **JOHN 10:10**

DAY THREE

This incredible salvation and freedom is a gift of God's grace.

day three

RECOGNIZING OUR SIN AND NEED FOR THE SAVIOR

Read Ephesians 2:1–9

Yesterday, we learned how God created a good and glorious world without sin and how humanity ruined this goodness with their disobedience. We also discussed how God put forth a plan to bring restoration and salvation from sin through Jesus Christ. However, it is possible for us to read about the Fall and God's promise and think, *What is the big deal? Is sin really that bad?* Just like Satan twisted God's words in the garden, so can he twist the truth about our sin. Satan can feed us lies that our sinful condition is nothing to worry about. He can even make us feel as if our sinful thoughts, desires, and actions are good things.

Sadly, this is why many people in our world today continue to live in sin without repentance. They are blind to the dangerous reality and repercussions of their sin. What these people — and those of us who doubt the seriousness of our sin — need is the gospel. When we come face to face with the gospel, we become painfully aware of our sinful condition and our need for a Savior. Ephesians 2:1–9 declares the gospel's good news, revealing the seriousness of our sin and the hope we have for our sin through Christ.

In Ephesians 2:1–3, the Apostle Paul describes our depravity. Paul does not make light of our sinfulness. Rather, he is crystal clear about who we were without Christ: we were dead. To be dead means that there was no true life in us. We may have had physical life, but we were heading toward spiritual death. Without Christ, we cannot truly live. Therefore, without Jesus, we are considered dead. Paul states that without Christ, we are dead in our trespasses and sins. These words describe the repetitious, deliberate disobedience against God that characterizes the life of an unbeliever.

Without Christ, we also walked according to the sinful ways of our world. Paul's use of the verb "walk" paints a picture of us taking steps toward what is wicked and participating in what opposes God and His law. Verse 2 also reveals how we walked according to Satan. Without Christ, we were essentially under Satan's authority. Satan controlled us, and the fact that we walked in the sinfulness of the world proves this to be true. Paul also writes in verse 3 that without Christ, we carried out the sinful desires of our flesh. Because we were under the control of Satan, we believed that following through with our desires and passions would lead us to joy and satisfaction. But doing so only perpetuated sin in our lives. For even if our desires brought us a semblance of happiness in the present, they would only bring death in the future.

> We did not bring about this salvation by our works—it is all by grace through faith in Christ.

Paul finishes this section of verses by describing the reality of our sinful condition, declaring that without Christ, we are "by nature children under wrath" (Ephesians 2:3). This means that because of our sin, we faced God's wrath. God's wrath is His righteous anger toward sin. We might not like the idea of God showing wrath, but God's wrath demonstrates His love, holiness, and justice. It is good that God opposes and punishes sin. If God were apathetic toward sin, He would not be a holy and loving God. Because God hates sin, His wrath will be poured out upon sinners in judgment.

The reality of our sinful condition should be sobering. The fact that we were once dead in our sins and deserved to be recipients of God's wrath should cause us to tremble. If Paul ended this passage here, with verse 3, we would be left without any hope for our depravity. However, Paul does continue, and his opening words in the next verse give us the encouragement we need. Like a burst of light in the darkness, these two words break through the hopelessness of our sinful condition: "but God." Even though we did not deserve to be rescued from our sin, God saved us out of His rich mercy and great love. Although we were dead in our sins, God made us alive in Christ. Through Christ's sacrifice on the cross and the grace we receive from Him, we are forgiven. We are saved from the punishment of our sins and given new life in Christ.

Verse 6 also reveals how we receive a position of glory in Christ. We are essentially taken out of the grave and placed on high with Jesus. Our position with Christ also means our authority changes through Christ's salvation. Because we are saved by Christ and brought into His kingdom, we are no longer under the control of Satan. Our allegiance changes, and our lives are now lived not for the wicked prince of this world but for the King of kings. Paul makes it known that this incredible salvation and freedom is a gift of God's grace. We did not bring about this salvation by our works—it is all by grace through faith in Christ.

Ephesians 2:1–9 opens our eyes to the reality of just how serious our sin truly is. Our sin keeps us from experiencing true and lasting life and only brings us pain and, ultimately, death. Though it may seem as if pursuing our sinful desires and delighting in sin will make us happy, today's passage reveals how sin only makes us broken and dead. So may the truth of our utter depravity lead us to the cross. May the reality of who we are without Christ drive us to our knees before the throne of God. And may the wondrous news of the gospel cause us to receive the salvation that is available through Christ. When our sin meets the Savior, our lives are forever changed.

> When our sin meets the Savior, our lives are forever changed.

day three reflection

How do you see our world downplay the seriousness of sin?

In what ways do you need to take your sin seriously?

How does God's intervention in your sinfulness humble you?

DAY FOUR

Part of living our lives for Christ involves us continuously turning away from our sins to pursue obedience to Christ.

day four

WALKING IN REPENTANCE

Read Proverbs 28:13, 1 John 1:9

Our salvation is a gift of grace we did not earn or deserve. However, there is action on our part that is necessary to receive this grace. The passage we looked at yesterday, Ephesians 2:1–9, certainly tells us that we are saved by grace, but it also says that we are saved by grace through faith (Ephesians 2:8).

Christ's death and resurrection must be something we believe for ourselves. We cannot know and experience Christ's grace and forgiveness if we do not trust and believe in who Jesus is and what He has done for us. How do we trust and believe in Christ? Paul, who wrote much of the New Testament, tells us in Romans 10:9–10, "If you confess with your mouth, 'Jesus is Lord,' and believe in your heart that God raised him from the dead, you will be saved. One believes with the heart, resulting in righteousness, and one confesses with the mouth, resulting in salvation."

The gospel is not something we are to only know in our minds; the gospel must be something we believe in our hearts. When we respond to the good news of the gospel through faith, we receive Christ's grace and forgiveness, and we become saved. This, too, is a gift from God, for we cannot come to believe in Christ unless the Holy Spirit opens our eyes to the truth, resulting in genuine belief.

However, coming to faith in Christ also involves repentance. Repentance is confessing our sins to the Lord and turning away from our sins to follow Christ. While repentance occurs at the time of salvation, it is also something we continue to do as believers. Part of living our lives for Christ involves us continuously turning away from our sins to pursue obedience to Christ.

Even though our salvation in Christ forgives our sin and frees us from our sin, we will still find ourselves tempted by sin. We will find that sinful desires and passions still swarm within us, although they do not control us. Because of this, we will sometimes stray away from Jesus, giving into our sinful desires and disobeying the Lord. But this is why repentance and confession are so important. When we come to the Lord in repentance, confessing our sins to Him, we place ourselves back on the path of obedience to Christ through the help of the Holy Spirit. Walking in repentance and confession is part of sanctification, which is our becoming more like Jesus.

However, knowing that repentance and confession are part of sanctification does not mean we will always seek to repent and confess. In fact, it is possible for us to be like Adam and Eve after the Fall, who hid from God and made excuses for their sin instead of confessing their sin to God (Genesis 3:8–13). Often, this hesitancy to repent and confess stems from fear and shame. Knowing that we have sinned does not feel good, and bringing these sins to the surface and exposing them before the Lord feels scary. In these moments, we are to remember the grace of our God.

As 1 John 1:9 tells us, God is faithful and righteous to forgive our sins when we confess them to Him. Therefore, we can come to God boldly with our sins. We can confess our sins to Him and turn away from them, knowing that we are forgiven. Remembering that we eternally belong to the Lord also encourages our repentance and confession. When we come to faith in Christ, we belong to Him forever. Nothing can separate us from God (Romans 8:35), and nothing can snatch us from His hand (John 10:28), even the sins we commit. So when we sin, we do not have to worry about the security of our salvation or fear that God is upset with us. Instead, we can remember our Father's faithfulness and our security in Him as we confidently confess our sins to Him.

Confessing our sins to other believers also sanctifies us. This, too, feels scary because it can be easy to fear how others will respond to our sins. We might worry that other believers will judge us or make us feel ashamed about the sins we confess. And while this response is possible, when we surround ourselves with believers who genuinely love the Lord and care about us, we need not be afraid to confess our sins to them. Having a community that loves us and gives us grace encourages us to confess our sins and struggles boldly. When we are honest about our sins with other believers, we receive the guidance and encouragement we need to walk in obedience to Christ.

And in the moments when we still struggle to confess our sins to God and others, we can rely on the Holy Spirit within us. The Holy Spirit comes to dwell within us when we come to faith in Christ. The Spirit aids us as we follow Jesus by convicting us of sin and empowering us to turn from sin to obey the Lord. Asking for the Spirit's help and relying on His power within us will give us the strength and confidence to confess to God and others. So even when repentance and confession seem hard or scary, we can remember the grace of our God, rely on the Spirit, and respond with humble and bold confession.

day four reflection

Read Romans 2:4. How does God's kindness lead us to repentance?

Read 2 Corinthians 7:8–10. What is the difference between godly grief over sin and worldly grief?

What sins do you need to confess to the Lord today? Spend some time confessing these sins to the Lord in prayer.

> *We can remember our Father's faithfulness and our security in Him as we confidently confess our sins to Him.*

Read Hebrews 4:14–16.

Reflect on this hymn and how it encourages or challenges you.

— Ways This Hymn Encourages Me —

— Ways This Hymn Challenges Me —

DAY FIVE

As followers of Jesus, we sacrifice everything for the One who sacrificed Himself for us.

day five

TAKING UP OUR CROSS

Read Mark 8:34–37

Have you ever heard someone use the expression "we all have a cross to bear" before? This saying is typically used when describing the troubles we all face and experience in our lives. These words reveal our human understanding that hardships are part of life and that we all must deal with them at some point. But in today's passage, we see Jesus use similar language in a different way. In Mark 8:34–37, Jesus declares how those who want to follow Him must be willing to deny themselves and take up their crosses. And while doing so does involve suffering, Jesus's words are more about sacrifice. As followers of Jesus, we sacrifice everything for the One who sacrificed Himself for us.

Unlike the saying "we all have a cross to bear," Jesus's words reveal the eternal significance and blessing of this life of sacrifice. Although being disciples of Christ comes with its challenges and hardships, living for Him brings joy. Why? Because when we follow Jesus, we receive abundant life. This is radically different from what the world believes and preaches. Our world teaches us that in order to experience joy and life, we must follow and delight in our passions and desires—we must do whatever makes us happy and fulfilled. But Jesus's words in Mark 8:34–37 say otherwise.

Jesus tells us that if we want to follow Him, we must deny ourselves. The translation of "to deny" in the original Greek means to affirm that one has no acquaintance with someone. We can think of Peter, for example, who denied that he knew Jesus three times during Christ's arrest (Matthew 26:69–75). Out of fear, Peter disassociated himself from Jesus. Similarly, we must disassociate ourselves from the sinful parts of ourselves if we want to follow Christ. We must not entertain our sinful selves but deny the parts of ourselves that want to pursue our sinful passions. Essentially, to deny ourselves is to deny our sinful nature—to say "no" to our sin and "yes" to who we are in Christ and how He wants us to live.

As followers of Christ, we must not only deny ourselves but also take up our crosses. The cross is a symbol of suffering and sacrifice. On the cross, Jesus sacrificed Himself in our place so that we could be forgiven for our sins. And Jesus experienced suffering to the point of death by His sacrifice. Because Jesus took up the cross for us, we can take up our cross for Him. In response to Christ's sacrifice for us, we are to make sacrifices for Him as believers. When we make a sacrifice, we give up something. In the Old Testament, the Israelites gave up their best animal to the Lord as a sacrifice (Leviticus 1:3). So, taking up our cross is connected to the command to deny ourselves. We live a life of sacrifice to the Lord by giving everything we have for Him, including our lives. This does not necessarily mean we will physically die for the Lord, but we are to spiritually die. We are to continuously put our sinful selves to death and walk in the new life Jesus gives us.

This is essentially what Jesus describes in Mark 8:35–36. In order to follow Jesus, we must lose our lives. If we cling tightly to what we want and desire—if we refuse to give up living for ourselves to instead live for Christ—we will not experience the eternal and abundant life Jesus offers us. If we live for ourselves, we will lose our lives in the end. But if we live for Christ by losing ourselves, we will gain life now and forever. Just as death was not the end for Christ, so death is not the end for us. If we are in Christ, we will spend eternity with the Lord. Like it was for Christ, our crosses will be traded for crowns when we step into eternity one day. Therefore, sacrificing for Christ and losing our lives for Him comes with a cost, but the cost is worth it because the gain is life abundant.

The Christian life is many things, but it is ultimately a life of sacrifice. Yet when we consider the abundant life that we receive in the present and the eternal life we will receive in the future, we will willingly take up our crosses. We will follow Jesus with joy, knowing that forsaking everything to follow Jesus is worth it.

But what does it look like to daily deny ourselves and take up our crosses? It looks like living for God's kingdom over the kingdom of this world, choosing to live for what God loves over what the world loves. It looks like resisting rather than listening to our desires that go against God and His kingdom. It looks like fixing our eyes on Jesus and not turning away from Him to follow other things. And it looks like persevering through suffering, knowing that we are being sanctified through every trial and trouble.

Following Jesus will be challenging because of our sinful nature, but with the help of the Holy Spirit, we are empowered to be disciples of Christ. As we rely on the Spirit, we have the strength we need to deny ourselves and pursue obedience to Christ. Although the road to glory involves suffering and sacrifice, we can pursue discipleship with perseverance. We can take up our crosses with joy rather than bear our crosses with grief because we know that, in Christ, we have true life.

day five reflection

In what ways do you need to deny yourself to follow Jesus?

How does knowing Jesus took up the cross for you
encourage you to take up your cross for Him?

What is currently keeping you from following Jesus more obediently?
What needs to be changed or removed from your life so that
you can follow Him obediently?

> With the help of the Holy Spirit,
> we are empowered to be disciples of Christ.

DAY SIX

When we set our minds on things above,
we focus on what is eternal
over what is temporal.

day six

SEEKING THE KINGDOM

Read Colossians 3:1–4

We are all focused on something in our daily lives. Perhaps we are focused on the kids we need to feed and prepare for school, the nine-to-five jobs we work, the degrees we are pursuing, or other regular roles and responsibilities. What we focus on the most reveals what we care about and love the most. And while it is good to diligently care for our families or be hard workers or students, God and His kingdom should be what we fixate on the most. In today's passage, the Apostle Paul encourages believers to seek the kingdom above all else in light of our position with and in Christ. To fully understand these directives, we first need to understand what it means to seek the kingdom; then, we will explore Paul's reasons for exhorting us to seek the kingdom above all else.

Before we get into today's passage, it is important to note that the directive to seek the kingdom of God first came from Jesus. In his Gospel, Matthew records Jesus's famous Sermon on the Mount (Matthew 5–7). In that sermon, Jesus directs His listeners to seek first God's kingdom and His righteousness (Matthew 6:33). Therefore, in Colossians 3:1–2, we see Paul echo Jesus's encouragement by breaking down this directive in two ways.

First, Paul encourages believers to "seek the things above" (Colossians 3:1). When we seek the things above, we choose to diligently pursue God and His kingdom. We focus our attention and devotion on what matters to the Lord. To set our minds on the things above involves an intentional orientation of our will. We orient our desires, thoughts, and affections toward God's kingdom and how we can serve His kingdom.

Second, Paul encourages believers to "set your minds on things above" (Colossians 3:2). When we set our minds on earthly things, we can become distracted by what does not matter and does not have eternal significance. We can get off track from following Jesus and end up living for the things of this world instead of Christ. But when we set our minds on things above, we focus on what is eternal over what is temporal. We declare that God's kingdom matters the most to us, and our lives match that declaration by the ways in which we live for the Lord.

In Colossians 3:1–4, Paul provides two reasons why we are to seek and set our minds on what is above. The first is because we have been raised with Christ (Colossians 3:1). As we have discussed, if we are in Christ, we have been brought from death to life. Through Christ's death and resurrection, we are raised to new life with Christ. But we have also been raised to a heavenly position with Christ. We learned this truth in Ephesians 2:6, and Paul seems to be speaking to this truth as well in Colossians 3:1. Even though we physically reside on earth, we spiritually live with Christ in heaven because we have a new position and home in Christ. As believers, our citizenship is in heaven (Philippians 3:20), and our identity is a heavenly one because we belong to Christ and His kingdom.

The second reason we are to seek and set our minds on what is above is because our sinful selves have died, and our lives are hidden with Christ in God (Colossians 3:3). There are two possible meanings for Paul's use of "hidden" in this verse. The first possible meaning is that even though we have a heavenly identity as believers, the full reality of that identity is hidden. This is likely why Paul follows up in Colossians 3:4 with the truth that we will appear with Christ in glory when He returns. One day, we will experience the full reality of what it looks like to be a citizen of heaven when Christ returns and glorifies us, transforming us into His likeness through the full removal of sin. Because this glorification is a future event, it is hidden for now.

Another possible meaning is that our lives are secure in God since "hidden" means to "hide in a safe place." Therefore, we can read this verse to mean that because we belong to God, He keeps us secure in His hands. Both possible interpretations reveal the security we have in the Lord and the hope for our future glorification.

Our identity and security in Christ, as well as our eternal blessings to come, motivate us to seek and set our minds on the things above. Knowing, remembering, and resting in who we are in Christ and our eternal future with Him encourages us to not focus on this temporal world. As we seek God's kingdom and aim to serve and please Him, we will not be as distracted or enthralled by the things of this world that have no eternal value. When we live as citizens of heaven, we forsake what is temporal to focus on the eternal.

However, consistently seeking and setting our minds on the things above will have its challenges. At times, we will find ourselves captivated by earthy things and more focused on the kingdom of this world than the kingdom of God. This is why we must be in God's Word daily and consistently be meditating on the gospel. When we read God's Word and dwell on the gospel, we are reminded of our heavenly identity and encouraged to set our minds on the things above once again.

This world will have its distractions and temptations, but we can live focused on Christ by seeking what is above and setting our minds on the things above. As we commit to living in this way, we will find our hearts, minds, and lives dedicated to and delighting in what matters most to the Lord. So let us live focused on our Savior and seek the kingdom that we are already members of in Christ.

> When we live as citizens of heaven, we forsake what is temporal to focus on the eternal.

day six reflection

Read Galatians 2:20. How does this verse describe the change in our devotion when we come to faith in Christ?

What keeps you from seeking first the kingdom of God?

What does it look like for you to practically set your mind on the things above?

DAY SEVEN

Christ's grace and forgiveness have freed us from sin and brought us from death to life.

day seven

PUTTING OFF AND PUTTING ON

Read Colossians 3:5–17

In yesterday's passage, we learned that we are to set our minds on the things above as we walk in this world as citizens of heaven. Today's passage continues to exhort us in the way we live as followers of Christ.

In Colossians 3:5–17, Paul provides two lists. The first is a list of sins we are to put off as believers. The second is a list of godly characteristics we are to put on. While these lists are not exhaustive, they reveal what we should refrain from and what we should pursue. In light of our heavenly position, we are to put off the sin we have been freed from and put on the characteristics of Christ.

Before Paul begins the list of sins, he gives us a command: "Put to death what belongs to your earthly nature" (verse 5). This language of putting to death connects with the theological term "mortification." Mortification involves killing the sin in our lives that springs up from our redeemed yet human hearts. Mortification is not a one-time event. As long as we live on this side of eternity, we must keep killing our sins. We can better understand mortification by thinking of tending to a flowerbed. You have to remove the weeds that will choke your plants and spray your plants to get rid of pesky bugs. But this maintenance needs to be regular in order to keep your plants healthy and growing. In the same way, we are to continuously put to death the sin in our lives. And with the power of the Lord, we are able to do so (1 Corinthians 10:13).

The word "therefore" at the beginning of verse 5 points us back to Paul's words in Colossians 3:1–4. As believers, we put to death the sins in our lives in response to our salvation in Christ. Christ's grace and forgiveness have freed us from sin and brought us from death to life. Living the Christian life does not involve turning back to the sin we have been released from. Rather, it involves killing that sin and pursuing obedience to Christ.

> Who we once were without Christ has died and has been replaced with who we now are in Christ.

Paul then lists out certain sins that are natural to our sinful flesh. As you read this list of sins, you may already feel convicted by some of them. In your own life, maybe you recognize the sin of anger because of the times you yell at your child or a loved one. Or perhaps you recognize the sin of greed because you spend too much money on the clothes you think will make you happy. While this list should alert us to our sins, its primary motivation is not to make us feel overwhelmed about our sins. Instead, it is meant to encourage us to press on in our sanctification as we put these sins to death through the power of the Spirit.

Paul provides this encouragement in verses 7 and 9–10. In verse 7, Paul reminds us that, as believers, these are sins we once walked in and lived in. Paul's words about these sins being what we once walked in remind us that we now walk in a different way of life. We used to walk in the ways of the world, but because of Christ, we are on a new path. We have been brought out of our sin and into Christ's righteousness. Therefore, in light of the righteousness we have received, we are to turn away from the sin we once lived in.

In verses 9–10, Paul reminds us that we have put off the old self and put on the new self. Who we once were without Christ has died and has been replaced with who we now are in Christ. Paul is specific that we have "put off the old self with its practices" (verse 9). What we once did when we lived as our old selves is not to be continued in our lives as believers. Putting on the new self involves pursuing a new way of living—a life dedicated to Christ. Paul also writes in verse 10 that we are being renewed as believers, which means that we have not yet been glorified. We are being sanctified in the present, little by little transforming more and more into the image of Christ. Because we are not yet glorified, our new selves will struggle against our old selves. However, knowing that we are being renewed gives us hope as we fight against sin and pursue obedience to God.

In verses 12–17, Paul encourages us in how we should live as believers. Like taking off dirty clothes and putting on clean clothes, so are we to put off sin and put on Christlikeness. Living like Christ involves being compassionate, kind, loving, and peaceful, among other qualities. We will look at the characteristics of Christ in more detail later in our study, but for now, these characteristics challenge how we live. This list contrasts greatly with the list in verses 5–9—and for good reason. How we live as believers should look drastically different from how we once lived apart from Christ.

Paul reminds us in verse 12 that we are God's chosen ones. God chose us as believers to receive the gift of salvation and new life. Therefore, as God's chosen ones, we are to live for Him. We are to walk forward in obedience instead of walking backward into disobedience. And we do so by putting off sin and putting on the characteristics of Christ with the Spirit's help. While this is a continual process as believers, we can have joy in this process as we consider our sanctification—our becoming more like Christ. Putting off our sins and putting on Christlikeness is not easy, but the Spirit will give us the perseverance and power we need to grow into the image of Christ.

> How we live as believers should look drastically different from how we once lived apart from Christ.

day seven reflection

In what ways are you living as your old self when
you are supposed to be living as your new self?

What can you do when putting sins to death is difficult?

Read over the list of Christlike actions in verses 12–15.
Spend some time in prayer, asking God to help you live out these actions.

DAY EIGHT

The Christian life is a life of sacrifice
that involves dying to ourselves
and living for the Lord.

day eight

LIVING SACRIFICES

Read Romans 12:1

What do you think of when you hear the word "sacrifice"? Maybe you think of the burnt offerings people used to (and sometimes still do) give to the gods they worship. Or perhaps you think of the personal sacrifices you make for the sake of others, such as cleaning the dishes even when you would rather not or playing with your children even when you had a long day of work. Both of these ideas are at play in Romans 12:1. In this verse, Paul calls us to be living sacrifices for the Lord. His words teach us how the Christian walk is a walk of daily sacrifice for the Lord. But what does this mean exactly, and what does it look like?

First, it is helpful to consider how sacrifices appear in Scripture. In the Old Testament, God's people would give sacrifices to the Lord. These sacrifices were usually animals, but they could also be grain offerings. God's people would offer up animals to be slaughtered or crops to be burned as actions of worship and thanksgiving. But sacrifices were also made as a way to atone for sins, or to have sins forgiven and cleared. When an Israelite gave a sin offering, the animal they provided would essentially take on their punishment through its death. The animal sacrifice would then symbolize the pardon of that person's sin and their relationship with God being made right.

However, God's people had to keep offering sacrifices in order to have their sins continually cleansed and their relationship with God restored. This is why God sent Jesus. Jesus sacrificed Himself once and for all on the cross so that those who trust and believe in Him will have their sins completely forgiven. Therefore, there is no need to keep offering sacrifices to the Lord for forgiveness because Christ is our ultimate sacrifice.

But just because we no longer have to offer physical sacrifices to receive God's grace does not mean we do not live sacrificially. As believers, we do not present animals to the Lord as sacrifices but our own bodies. And while this does not involve a sacrificial physical death, it does involve a sacrificial spiritual death. As we learned from Mark 8:34–37, the Christian life is a life of sacrifice that involves dying to ourselves and living for the Lord. Therefore, we live as living sacrifices by daily obeying the Lord, even at the cost of our own wants and desires.

Paul also teaches us that presenting ourselves as living sacrifices is our true worship. Sacrifices in the Bible were acts of repentance and thanksgiving but also acts of worship. Sacrifices were seen as a display of praise and worship to the Lord, the one true God. In the same way, being a living sacrifice is an act of worship. As followers of Christ, we live sacrificially as a means to glorify and honor the Lord. We desire our thoughts, words, and actions to give glory to God and please Him. So while singing songs of praise to God is certainly part of worship, our true worship is giving our whole selves sacrificially to the Lord.

In our day-to-day lives, this true worship is displayed by the ways that we seek to be holy in all that we say and do. Presenting ourselves as living sacrifices involves living for the Lord and not ourselves, speaking words, and having actions that honor the Lord. This kind of living connects with what we read in yesterday's passage, where Paul instructs us, "And whatever you do, in word or in deed, do everything in the name of the Lord Jesus, giving thanks to God the Father through him" (Colossians 3:17). When we do everything to serve and honor the Lord, we live as living sacrifices. Our lives are dedicated to worshiping and glorifying the Lord in all that we say and do.

> Our true worship is giving our whole selves sacrificially to the Lord.

However, worshiping the Lord with all of who we are is hard. As followers of Christ, we still battle sinful desires that pull us away from obeying the Lord. And we live in a world that tempts us to worship other things. If we are not worshiping the Lord, we are worshiping something else. This is called idolatry, and idols can spring up in our lives in the form of things like materialism or security. So as believers, we may desire to worship the Lord but find in ourselves a tension between worshiping Him and other things. What helps us in this tension is remembering why we are to worship the Lord.

Paul tells us in Romans 12:1 that it is "in view of the mercies of God" that we are to present ourselves as living sacrifices. As believers, we live worshipful lives in light of God's mercies. With the Spirit's help, we remember and rejoice over God's gift of salvation through Christ and His great mercy to forgive us, even though we are sinners. Dwelling on God's mercies reminds us of what we have received through Christ, what we are receiving through Christ, and what we will one day receive through Christ.

In response to such mercies, we give all of ourselves in sacrificial worship to the Lord through the Spirit's power. So in the moments when we find ourselves struggling to worship the Lord rightly, we can remember God's mercies. We can meditate on all that God has done for us and given to us through Christ and allow those truths to humble our hearts and encourage our devotion. The more we remember and rest in God's mercies, the more we will worship the Lord with all of who we are.

> As believers, we live worshipful lives in light of God's mercies.

day eight reflection

Read Deuteronomy 6:4–5. What does it look like to personally love God with all your heart, soul, and strength?

What obstacles do you experience when it comes to worshiping the Lord?

How does considering Christ's sacrifice for you encourage you to present yourself as a living sacrifice?

DAY NINE

God's Word calls us to be holy in every area of our lives.

day nine

PURSUING HOLINESS

Read 1 Peter 1:13–21

Yesterday's passage exhorted us to worship God with all of who we are. While our worship is ultimately for the Lord, our worship also impacts us as followers of Christ. When we daily glorify the Lord with our thoughts, words, and actions, we grow in sanctification. As we have noted, sanctification is the process by which we become more and more like Christ. To become more like Christ is to grow in holiness since Christ is perfectly holy. Today's passage encourages us as believers to pursue holiness as we live on this earth, reflecting the One who is the definition of holiness.

First, it is helpful to understand what it means to be holy. To be holy means to be pure and set apart, specifically from evil and unrighteousness. As believers, we are already positionally holy because of Christ. Through Christ's grace and forgiveness, we are pure because we have been cleansed from our sin and deemed innocent of our sin. Our salvation in Christ makes us set apart, as we now belong to Christ and God's kingdom. But we are also set apart because Christ has given us His righteousness, causing us to be separated from the unrighteousness that once ruled over us and in us. While we are positionally holy because of Jesus, we are still progressively being made holy. We are daily putting off sin and seeking to walk in obedience. One day, we will become completely holy when Christ returns, but right now, we are being transformed from one degree of glory to the next (2 Corinthians 3:18, ESV).

This pursuit of holiness involves not being conformed to our previous sinful desires. To be conformed to these desires is to follow after them and live for them. However, Jesus rescued us from the desires of our former ignorance; therefore, we are not to turn back to this way of living. Instead, we are to pursue God's will and commands, knowing that we have been set free from our previous way of life (1 Peter 1:14). Peter also says that we are God's "obedient children" in verse 14 and reminds us in verse 15 how we have been called by God. To be called by God and declared a child of God points us to God's love and grace to take us out of sin and death and bring us to Himself.

> Knowing that we have been redeemed by Christ's blood should motivate us to pursue and walk in holiness.

As children of God, we are to reflect our heavenly Father. Peter writes in verses 15–16 that we are to be holy because God is holy. Just as little children may imitate their father, so are we to imitate our heavenly Father in our conduct. Being holy like God is holy can seem like an impossible task. After all, God is the only One who is truly holy. But even though we are growing in our holiness on this side of eternity, we can be holy as God is holy by resisting sin and delighting in who God is through the Spirit's power. As we aim to worship the Lord daily and obey His good commands, we will grow to look more like the holy God we serve. Peter makes it clear in verse 15 that we are to be holy in all of our actions. We may aim to be holy in some areas of our lives, but God's Word calls us to be holy in every area of our lives.

In the remaining verses, Peter provides more reasons why we should live holy lives as believers. Verse 17 reveals how we are to conduct ourselves in reverence because of God's judgment, or discipline. Even though we are justified by grace through faith in Christ, our works will be evaluated by God when we stand before Him one day. We do not have to fear this day or believe that our present works maintain our favor with God. But knowing that God will evaluate what we do should challenge us in the way we live. And knowing that God currently sees what we do should also challenge us in our conduct. What we do is not hidden from the Lord. Therefore, we are not to live as children who try to hide their actions from their father. Instead, we are to allow our fear of the Lord—our respect and reverence for who God is and how He calls us to live—to motivate our holy conduct.

Peter also reminds us of the redemption we have received from Christ (1 Peter 1:18–19). God rescued and set us free from our empty, meaningless way of life. Therefore, we are to live in this new life He has given us instead of going back to our old way of life. Knowing that we have been redeemed by Christ's blood should motivate us to pursue and walk in holiness. The precious blood of Christ was shed for us. This amazing truth reminds us of the great cost of our redemption and should sober us. Christ came for us and died for us, enabling us to become forgiven and holy. In response to His sacrifice for us, we are to live holy lives out of humility and gratitude.

As Peter concludes this passage, He reminds us that our hope and faith are in God through Christ. This final truth encourages our hearts as we seek to be holy. At times, pursuing holiness is difficult. Saying "no" to sin and "yes" to righteousness will sometimes feel like drudgery rather than delight. But when we remember that our hope and faith are in God, we remember our utter dependence on Him. God will give us the strength we need to pursue holiness. After all, the One who is perfectly holy gives us the power to reflect His holiness. Therefore, we can depend on Him as we aim to walk in holiness. We can trust in the Lord as He transforms us into the holy people we were always meant to be.

> We can trust in the Lord as He transforms us into the holy people we were always meant to be.

day nine reflection

Read Psalm 119:9. How does God's Word
help us grow in purity and holiness?

How are you currently reflecting your holy Father?

How can you pursue holiness daily?

DAY TEN

To walk by the Spirit is to produce
the fruit of the Spirit.

day ten

WALKING BY THE SPIRIT

Read Galatians 5:16–26

Imagine you are going on a walk with a friend. You would not walk behind or in front of your friend but alongside them. Your walk would also likely have a designated path and destination. You both would know where you are going and which direction you need to walk in order to reach that destination.

As believers, living the Christian life is like walking with a friend, except this friend is the Lord. On day five of our study, we discussed how we are to follow Jesus. And while Christ is ahead of us, leading and guiding us toward eternity, He is also alongside us. With the Holy Spirit dwelling within believers, we have the Spirit of God with us always. And as the Holy Spirit indwells us, we are to walk by the Spirit as we go about our everyday lives. In Galatians 5:16–26, we see a picture of what this walk looks like.

Paul begins this passage with an encouragement: if we walk by the Spirit, we will not carry out our fleshly desires (Galatians 5:16). However, the next verse can seem somewhat discouraging. In Galatians 5:17, Paul describes how our fleshly desires are opposed to the Spirit's desires. It is as if our desires and the Spirit's desires are at war, and we find ourselves stuck in this battle. If you are in Christ, you likely know this struggle well. You know what it is like to know that you should obey the Spirit's instruction and guidance but want to go your own way instead. You know what it is like to find yourself giving into your fleshly desires, even though you know that it is the opposite of what the Spirit desires. While this tension and battle can be overwhelming and even discouraging, the truth of verse 16 meets us in this struggle. Even though we wrestle against our flesh, we can have hope that when we walk by the Spirit, we will not pursue our fleshly desires.

Such truth reminds us of the help and power of the Holy Spirit. As believers, we have been given the Holy Spirit to aid us in our walks with Christ. The Holy Spirit is active in our sanctification by convicting us of sin, empowering us to resist temptation, and enabling us to pursue obedience to Christ. Although we feel weak in our fight against our fleshly desires, the Spirit is strong within us. When we walk by the Spirit, we will experience the strength we need to fight against and not give in to our sinful desires. But what exactly does it look like to walk by the Spirit?

Walking by the Spirit is living as God has called us to live rather than living like we once were before we came to know Christ. In Galatians 5:19–21, we receive a list of the works of the flesh that we are not to pursue. Similar to the list in Colossians 3:5–9, this list reveals how we are not to partake in sins such as sexual immorality, division, and drunkenness. Though we will all fail and give into sin from time to time, the sins listed in these verses should not be a regular pattern in our lives as believers.

Paul warns in Galatians 5:21 that those who practice these sins will not inherit God's kingdom. While this is a weighty warning, it should not cause us to be afraid as believers. As mentioned above, we will all sin from time to time, even as believers, and thankfully, there is forgiveness in Christ for us when we do. However, what Paul is discussing in Galatians 5:21 is something different—here, he is addressing those who walk in and practice these works of the flesh continually with no repentance. This continual, unrepentant sin may reveal that someone is not a true follower of Jesus, and those who are not followers of Jesus will not inherit the kingdom of God.

However, if you truly trust in Jesus and desire to walk in His ways, even though you will sin, you do not have to fear that sinning will keep you from inheriting God's kingdom. If you are in Christ, you will always belong to God's kingdom. And knowing that we belong to God's kingdom encourages us not to pursue the works of the flesh but the fruit of the Spirit instead.

In verses 22–26, we receive a list of the fruit of the Spirit. As believers, this is the fruit that flourishes within us as we are sanctified, and it should be evident in our words and actions. Therefore, to walk by the Spirit is to produce the fruit of the Spirit. Rather than resisting how the Spirit encourages us to live, we are to be obedient to the Spirit's conviction, resulting in us bearing fruit for the Lord. We know that we are walking by the Spirit through the ways the fruit of the Spirit is displayed in our lives. In our struggle against sin, we can be encouraged by the ways we see fruit—such as love, kindness, and self-control—produced in our everyday lives.

Paul also provides us with more encouragement as we seek to turn away from our sinful desires in verse 24, which reads, "Now those who belong to Christ Jesus have crucified the flesh with its passions and desires." This truth reminds us that our sinful flesh has been spiritually put to death. How? Through Jesus's sacrifice on the cross. As Paul writes in Galatians 2:20a, "I have been crucified with Christ, and I no longer live, but Christ lives in me." Our old, sinful selves are gone, and we have been brought to new life in Christ. So while we still battle against the desires of our flesh, we can be encouraged by the reminder that our fleshly desires have been defeated in Christ. Our flesh may still tempt us, but our fleshly desires cannot control or overtake us.

Knowing that our fleshly desires have been killed reminds us that Christ has transformed the way we live. Therefore, we are able to live out the fruit of the Spirit because we have been transformed by Christ and because we have His Spirit dwelling within us. We live by the Spirit because Christ has made us new. In light of this truth, let us seek to live by the Spirit and keep in step with the Spirit. Let us continue to walk by the Spirit as He leads us toward eternity.

> We live by the Spirit because Christ has made us new.

day ten reflection

Why should we walk by the Spirit as believers?

How do you see the fruit of the Spirit evident in your life?

How can you keep in step with the Spirit?

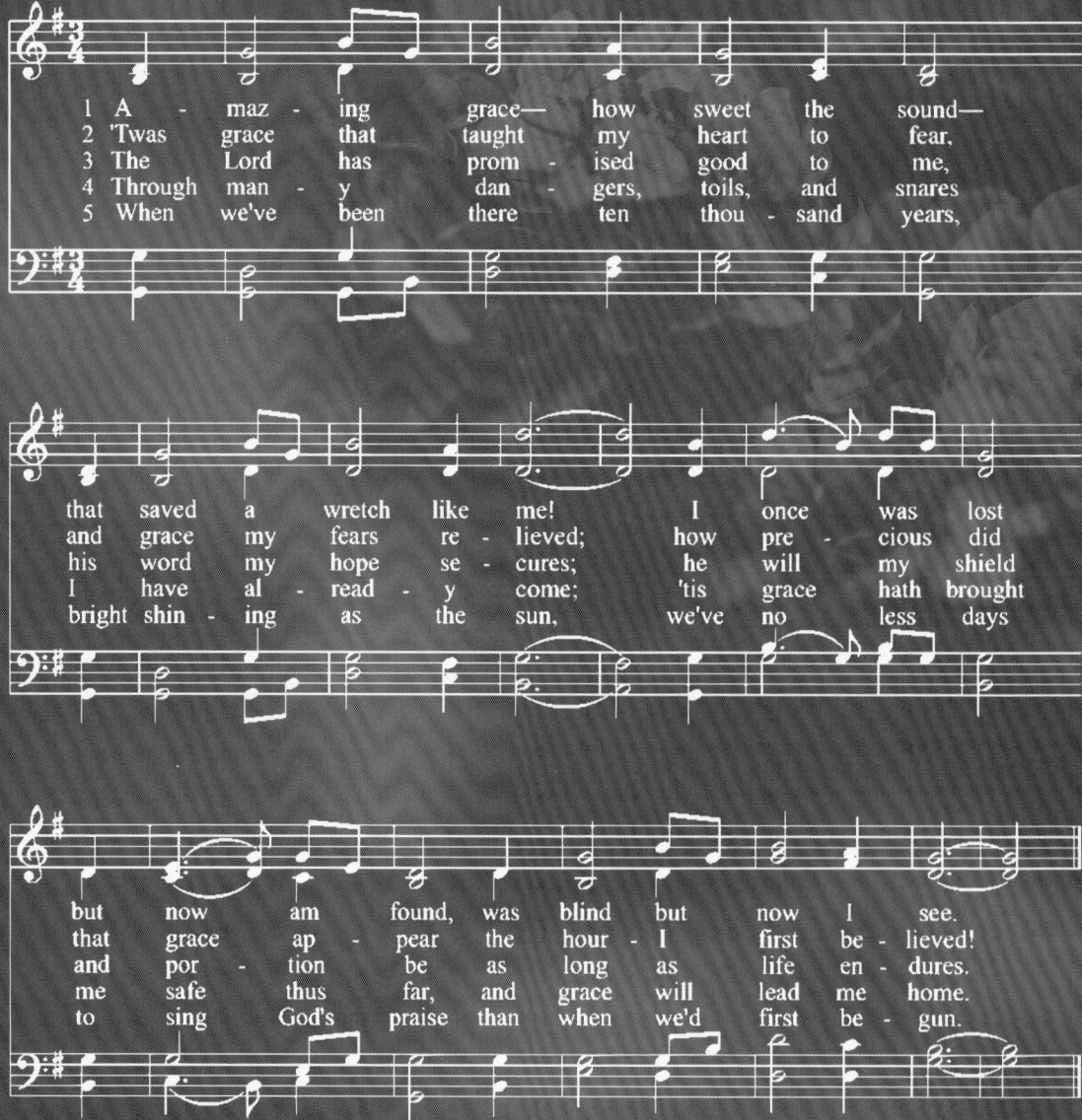

Read Ephesians 2:1–10.

Reflect on this hymn and how it encourages or challenges you.

Ways This Hymn Encourages Me

Ways This Hymn Challenges Me

02 part two

The Sins We Wrestle With

DAY ELEVEN

Jesus not only forgives our sin
but transforms our lives.

day eleven

CONSIDERING OUR SIN

Read 1 John 1:5–10

In part one, we discussed the seriousness of our sin and how Jesus not only forgives our sin but transforms our lives. However, it is important for believers to recognize that though we are daily being transformed into Christ's image, we still wrestle with sin. Therefore, we continue the difficult but necessary fight against sin. And an important part of fighting against our sin is recognizing the sins we wrestle with. When we recognize and repent from our sin—with the help of the Spirit—we grow more into the image of Christ.

Throughout this next part, we will walk through various sins we wrestle with as believers. Knowing that this is what lies ahead might fill us with fear. It is not easy to come face to face with our sin. Doing so can make us feel grieved, ashamed, and perhaps even dirty. While it is good for us to recognize our sin and its seriousness, it is also important that we rest in Christ's grace. If we are in Christ, we have Christ's grace and mercy no matter the sins we wrestle with. Our feelings of shame and fear are always met with Christ's love and forgiveness.

Even though we will discuss different sins in this section of the study, we will also look to the hope that Jesus provides us for these sins. Doing so will give us the encouragement we need to keep fighting our sin. We may struggle with sin on this side of eternity, but Christ meets us in our struggle with sin. As we look to Him and the truth of the gospel, we will not be afraid to confront our sin. Instead, we will boldly face and fight our sin, knowing that Jesus is on our side.

day eleven reflection

Journal below any feelings you may have about considering the sins you wrestle with. End in prayer, asking God to fix your eyes on the gospel as you go through this next part.

DAY TWELVE

Help and hope are found when
we come to Christ with our unbelief.

day twelve

MOVING FROM UNBELIEF TO BELIEF

Read Mark 9:14–29

I do not believe God is good.

There is no way God could love me.

I do not think God wants what is best for me.

What does it mean about us if we struggle with these types of doubts? Does this mean that we are bad Christians? Does this mean that we are not actually saved? These kinds of doubts and thoughts can lead us to believe different things about ourselves, but they ultimately reveal unbelief in our hearts. Even after we trust in Christ for our salvation, we can find ourselves wrestling with unbelief, causing us to doubt who God is and even pull away from God altogether.

The Sin of Unbelief

When we experience unbelief, we struggle to believe what God's Word says about who God is, what He has done, and what He will do. We do this by doubting God's character in the midst of fear or doubting that God will come through for us in troubling circumstances. Recognizing unbelief as a sin can make us squirm, especially because of how easy it can be to not trust the Lord. But Mark 9:14–29 reminds us that help and hope are found when we come to Christ with our unbelief.

From Death to Life

The father in Mark 9:14–29 recognizes his belief in Jesus, but his belief is small. This is why he cries to Jesus, "I do believe; help my unbelief!" (verse 24). Remarkably, Jesus does not wait until the father no longer struggles with unbelief to help his son. He heals even with the presence of unbelief. Jesus's mercy in this moment gives us hope in our own struggles with unbelief. We might believe that we have to have perfect faith in order for God to work in our lives. We might even fear that bad things will happen in our lives because we do not have enough faith. Scripture confronts us in these fears by reminding us that God works in and through us even when we struggle with unbelief.

Consider the ways in which God remained faithful to the Israelites, even though they doubted Him and turned away from Him time and time again. Or consider Jesus's patience with His disciples, even though they constantly failed in their faith (Luke 8:23–25, Luke 24:1–12, John 20:24–29). God's faithfulness is not dependent on the size of our faith. He will continue to move and work, even when we wrestle with doubt.

We also see in Mark 9:14–29 that we can ask God to help us in our unbelief. The father's cry for help reveals his understanding that Jesus could strengthen his faith. This man could have tried to hide his unbelief from Jesus, but he was honest with Jesus about his struggle. What would it look like to have the same response? What would it look like to humbly and honestly come to the Lord with our unbelief? Perhaps it would look like pouring out all of our worries and doubts to God, knowing that God is a faithful Father who listens to His children.

> God's faithfulness is not dependent on the size of our faith.

However, the doubts and the thoughts of unbelief that we can wrestle with might cause us to move further away from the Lord. This is why we must remember the gospel. The gospel reminds us that we have Christ's forgiveness, no matter our struggle with doubt. Because there is no condemnation for those in Christ (Romans 8:1), we are welcome to go to God with our unbelief without any fear of chastisement. So when doubts creep into our minds or when we struggle to believe a particular truth about God's character, we can rest in God's grace.

Resting in Christ's grace looks like not trying to increase our faith through sheer willpower. It looks like meditating on God's character, dwelling on God's goodness and faithfulness. It looks like slowing down and remembering what is true because of Christ. As we rest in what Christ has accomplished for us, we find freedom to delight in His grace, trusting in Him as He deepens and grows our faith.

Though we may wrestle with unbelief from time to time, unbelief is a struggle we can take to God. God invites us to Himself and desires to help us in our unbelief. Will we go to Him?

day twelve reflection

How do you struggle with unbelief?

How do the truths from Mark 9:14–29
encourage you in your unbelief?

Write a prayer to the Lord, confessing to Him any areas
of unbelief and asking Him to fuel your faith.

> As we rest in what Christ has accomplished for us, we find freedom to delight in His grace.

DAY THIRTEEN

Anything we worship besides God keeps us from becoming who God created us to be.

day thirteen

WORSHIPING GOD OVER EVERYTHING ELSE

Read Exodus 20:3–6, Jonah 2:8–9

What comes to mind when you see the word "idolatry"? Typically, images of a golden calf or people bowing down to some kind of image or statue fill our minds. And while these pictures do represent idolatry, idolatry is so much more than bowing down to a physical object or image. Idolatry is anything we place before God and give our main attention and adoration. It always involves worshiping what is created and temporal instead of the God who is self-existent and eternal. Rather than being idolatrous, God's Word calls us to worship God alone and give Him our utmost devotion.

The Sin of Idolatry

We might think, *I do not struggle with idolatry*, but idolatry presents itself in ways that often go unnoticed by us. For example, relationships might be an idol for us if we see a person or group of people as what we need to feel affirmed or satisfied. Alternatively, money might be an idol for us if we are constantly worried about our finances and feel like we need to have a certain amount of money to feel secure. The things we often think about and care about reveal the idols in our lives.

God created us to worship Him alone (Exodus 20:3–6). God created us to adore Him above all else and have Him be the main focus of our lives. But when we worship something other than God, we become formed by that thing. Anything we worship besides God keeps us from becoming who God created us to be. Idolatry also causes us to rely on something to give us what only God can give. Idolatry causes us to essentially put something else on the throne of our hearts instead of God.

From Death to Life

Our sinful tendency to worship idols is grave, but thankfully, God sent us Jesus to fix our worship problem. Jesus is the perfect example of what true worship of God looks like. Jesus never wavered in His worship of the Father, even when He faced strong temptation (Matthew 4:8–10). But Jesus did not come only to show us what true worship looks like—He came to *make us* true worshipers. Jesus's sacrifice on the cross cleanses the sin of idolatry in our hearts and restores our relationship with God. With our sins forgiven, our hearts made new, and our relationship with God restored, we are able to worship the Lord as we were created to do.

However, this does not mean that we will worship God perfectly on this side of eternity. As believers, idolatry can still be a problem and often causes us to struggle in our devotion to the Lord. Our struggle to worship God alone as believers is certainly difficult, but we do not have to despair. Why? Because we are not alone in our worship struggle. Christ has given us the Spirit to help us combat idolatry.

With the Spirit's help, we are able to recognize when we are worshiping idols, and we are given the strength to turn away from this worship. The Spirit enables us to "flee from idolatry" (1 Corinthians 10:14) by removing idols in our lives and keeping our worship of the Lord central.

But are we relying on the Spirit? Or are we trying to fix our idolatry problem on our own? When we try to fix our idolatry problem on our own, we will find ourselves frustrated. After all, even if we removed every single thing that kept us from worshiping God, we would still be left with the deeper issue at hand. We cannot rid ourselves of our desire for attention, security, pleasure, or whatever it may be that leads us to idolatry. Only God can uproot the idols of our hearts and give us what we look for in the things of this world.

Consider how much our hearts would remain focused on and devoted to the Lord if we daily relied on the Spirit. Consider how our worship would be shaped if we regularly spent time in God's Word, prayed, praised God, and walked in obedience with the Spirit's help. The more we depend on the Spirit to help us worship God, the more we are kept from worshiping anything apart from Him.

day thirteen reflection

What are the idols in your life?

Why are these things idols?

Read and meditate on Psalm 115:1–8.
Journal any thoughts about these verses below.

> "Only God can uproot the idols of our hearts."

DAY FOURTEEN

We are to love all people
because Christ loved all people.

day fourteen

TRADING APATHY FOR MERCY

Read Luke 10:25–37, 1 John 3:17–18

Have you ever seen someone in need and hesitated to help them? Sometimes we can make excuses for why we fail to help others. *I am too busy. Someone else will probably help them. They can probably figure things out themselves.* While we cannot help every person in every situation, lacking care and compassion for others is called apathy—and apathy is a sin. Rather than being apathetic, as believers, we are called to reflect Christ by caring for and helping those in need to the best of our ability.

The Sin of Apathy

What does apathy look like? Apathy looks like seeing a homeless person begging for money and feeling no desire to help them. It looks like hearing about a disaster in another country and not giving a second thought about those who have been harmed. It can also look like choosing not to pray for someone who is struggling or in need. Apathy always involves an absence of concern.

We see apathy on display in Jesus's parable of the Good Samaritan. The first two men in the story are a priest and Levite. Priests and Levites held important roles in the temple during Jesus's day, so one might easily assume that these men would help. But the two men avoid the hurt man. Perhaps they do so to uphold the purity laws of the Old Testament and avoid making themselves ceremonially unclean (Leviticus 21:1). But even then, they could still ensure this man has the help he needs. They could make sure someone else assists the man. They could speak to the man and assure him that they would not leave him alone. Instead, they cross over to the side of the road and leave the man to die. Thankfully, a third person stops to help. But this person is someone who would have been completely unexpected to Jesus's first-century Jewish audience.

From Death to Life

The third person is a Samaritan. Samaritans and Jews had a long history of tension between them. Yet, this Samaritan goes right to the man and tends to his wounds. He even goes above and beyond by bringing the man to an inn and paying for his stay. Though it is the opposite of what Jesus's original audience would have expected, this Samaritan shows immense compassion.

This parable on radical mercy comes after Jesus tells an expert in the Law to love God and his neighbor (Luke 10:27–28). This expert in the Law asks, "Who is my neighbor?" (Luke 10:29) as a way to justify himself and narrow the scope of who he should love. But Jesus's parable teaches a different approach. As believers, we should not ask, "Who should I love?" but "How can I love?" We are to not love only some people but all people. We are to love all people because Christ loved all people.

Christ moved toward the hurting. He had compassion for the lost. He willingly healed the sick. Jesus always showed mercy, so much so that He died on the cross. Christ demonstrated His immense compassion toward us by dying for us. Christ demonstrated His radical mercy by giving up His life on the cross. He did not leave us to die in our sins. He did not see our need for salvation and feel no desire to intervene. Jesus is the true Good Samaritan.

> Jesus transforms our apathy into mercy.

How much would our hearts change if we saw people through the eyes of Christ? We would be encouraged to stop instead of hurrying on. We would be challenged not to make excuses. We would be motivated to show others mercy with gladness. Considering Christ's love for others compels our own love for others. The more we remember Christ's mercy and love, the more our hearts grow warm with compassion. Jesus transforms our apathy into mercy.

It is God's love in us that moves us toward people. It is through our actions that we display God's mercy (1 John 3:17–18). So let us reflect our Savior by being quick to love, help, and show mercy. May our compassion and care for others point to the compassionate and caring God we serve.

day fourteen reflection

How are you prone to be apathetic?
What is at the root of your apathy?

In what ways does God's love impact your apathy?

Meditate on Romans 12:9–11.
How can you live out the actions in these verses?

> May our compassion and care for others
> point to the compassionate
> and caring God we serve.

DAY FIFTEEN

Believers are called to love both God and others, and we cannot love God while simultaneously hating others.

day fifteen

TURNING HATRED INTO LOVE

Read 1 John 4:7–11, 20–21

"I hate you!" A little boy screams at his mother and slams the door. Even if these words were spoken without true intent, they can still pierce the hearts of those who receive them. While we can use the word "hate" jokingly or without thinking, "hate" is a strong word—and hatred is a sin. Hatred goes beyond apathy to an extreme dislike of someone, and it typically involves exhibiting cruel behavior toward them because of this dislike. Hatred is not of God. Furthermore, as believers, hating others fails to reflect the God of love whom we serve.

The Sin of Hatred

Hatred is often rooted in another sin. For example, we may hate someone because we are jealous of them. Or we might hate someone because of something they did to us; perhaps a person deeply hurt or wronged us, and we feel burning hatred toward them. Pride can also lead to hatred, as we can hate others because we believe we are superior to them. We should be mindful of these sins as believers and repent of them so that they do not sprout hatred within us.

Believers are called to love both God and others, and we cannot love God while simultaneously hating others. When we love God rightly, we love others rightly. Therefore, if we hate others, we fail to love God as we should. If we hate people who are made in the image of God, we essentially do not love the One whose image is upon them (1 John 4:20). This truth might make us uncomfortable, but it is good for us to realize that our love of God and our love of others go hand in hand.

From Death to Life

It is imperative that, as believers, we image God rightly by loving all people. This does not mean that we have to agree with all people or affirm all that people do, but we should love others no matter who they are or what they have done. Why? Because love is from God, and God is love (1 John 4:7–8). If we have been saved by the God of love, we are to reflect His love. How? By putting others before ourselves. By being kind and compassionate. By treating people with respect as the image-bearers they are. When we love others, we reflect the One who is the very definition of love.

What's more, when we love others, we reflect not only God but the gospel as well. God chose to pursue us out of His love, and He gave us Jesus, who forgives our sins even though we are sinners. Therefore, as believers, the love we show others points to the love of God through Christ. And when we love others sacrificially, we reflect Christ's sacrificial love on the cross. We reflect Jesus's sacrificial love when we choose to love others even when it is costly.

Regularly dwelling on the gospel keeps hatred from taking root. When we meditate on the gospel, we are reminded of God's love for us in Christ. We are reminded how we have been deeply loved, even though we do not deserve to receive such love. The more and more we reflect on the gospel, the more love grows inside of us. The fires of hatred are extinguished by the waters of the gospel.

God invites us to come to Him with our struggle to love. We do not have the power to squash our hatred ourselves. We do not have the strength to keep hatred away on our own. As we regularly go to the Lord, asking Him to remove any semblance of hatred within us, we will receive help as God changes our hearts. Because God is a God of love, He empowers His children to reflect His love.

Jesus once said that the world will know that we are His disciples by our love (John 13:35). With this truth in mind, let us commit ourselves to show the love of Christ. Hatred may exist in our world, but may it not exist in the hearts of God's people. May the love of God — displayed brightly through Christ and His sacrifice — shine in the hearts and lives of every follower of Christ.

day fifteen reflection

Why is hate contrary to the gospel?

How can you keep hatred from growing within you?

Meditate on Romans 5:8 and John 3:16.
Record your thoughts below on how these verses
encourage your love in light of God's love.

> When we love others,
> we reflect the One who is
> the very definition of love.

DAY SIXTEEN

Through Christ's sacrifice,
we receive blessing upon blessing.

day sixteen

FORGOING GREED FOR TRUE SATISFACTION

Read Mark 10:23–31, Luke 12:13–21

As humans, we naturally want more and more of what makes us happy. This desire can be for something simple and sweet, such as more time spent with a loved one or extra time being cozy in bed. But this desire can become sinful when wanting more is rooted in greed. Greed is a selfish and insatiable need for something, such as fame or fortune. A byproduct of greed is materialism, which involves purchasing and clinging to physical possessions as a means of comfort or happiness. Greed and materialism can easily worm themselves into our hearts no matter our material wealth—whether we have plenty or little. While it can be hard to realize our tendency to be greedy, when we recognize and repent of these sins, we are able to cling to God alone.

The Sin of Greed

Greed is a sin because our greed causes us to disbelieve that God is all we need. When we disbelieve that God is all we need, we can rely on money to be what only God can be for us. It is not wrong to earn and save money, but we become greedy when wealth becomes something we ultimately live for. Greed occurs when we revolve our lives around money rather than the Lord. As a result, we can turn money into an idol and essentially worship money through our relentless pursuit of and need for it.

Furthermore, greed that leads to materialism causes us to depend on physical items more than God. When we are being materialistic, we view physical possessions as our ultimate source of happiness and security. In doing so, we can keep buying items in order to maintain this sense of satisfaction. While it is not wrong to purchase something we like or enjoy a certain possession, relying on these things as our source of satisfaction is sinful. Materialism essentially causes us to say to God, "I do not need You," and try to rely on created things to give us the life and the joy that the Creator ultimately provides in Himself.

From Death to Life

Our lives and our joy are not found in the abundance of possessions (Luke 12:15). Our lives and our joy are found in Jesus, who gives us abundantly more than what this world offers. Possessions and money will not last. Therefore, we do not have to place our security and identity in something that is temporal. Instead, we can place our security and identity in Jesus, who is eternal. In Christ, we have what we need. In Christ, we have spiritual blessings that far outweigh money and physical possessions.

Therefore, followers of Jesus are the ones who are truly rich. Believers may or may not have lots of money on this side of eternity, but they will gain eternal blessings in heaven. These eternal blessings are not material blessings, like jewels or gold; these eternal blessings are Jesus Himself and a life spent with Him in a world of peace forever.

What would it look like to care more about the riches we have in Christ over the riches of this world? Rather than seeing an ad for a particular item and buying it for our happiness, we might choose to dwell on the joy we have in Christ instead. When we feel that impulse to gain more money in order to feel secure, we might spend some time in prayer, thanking God for being our true source of security. In the moments when we want our closets to be filled with more and more, we might choose to dwell on the truth that no earthly item can satisfy our deepest desires.

Through Christ's sacrifice, we receive blessing upon blessing. We receive the blessing of forgiveness from sin, a new life, a future home with Christ, everlasting peace, and so much more. In Christ, we have exactly what we need. When we remember that all we need is Christ and we have all we need in Christ, we will not be greedy or materialistic. We will be thankful and content with what we have instead of desiring to have more and more.

day sixteen reflection

In what ways can you be greedy?
What can you do to keep yourself from being greedy?

Read Matthew 6:19–21.
How do these verses challenge you?

Write a prayer below, confessing to God any areas of greed in your life.
Ask God to help you see Him as all that you need and help you
focus on Christ's spiritual blessings over the riches of this world.

> "In Christ, we have exactly what we need."

Come, Ye Sinners, Poor and Needy

Joseph Hart

1 Come ye sin-ners, poor and nee-dy, Weak and woun-ded,
2 Come, ye thir-sty, come and wel-come, God's free boun-ty
3 Come ye wea-ry, hea-vy-la-den, Lost and ru-ined
4 Let not cons-cience make you lin-ger, Nor of fit-ness

sick and sore; Je-sus read-y stands to save you,
glo-ri-fy; True be-lief and true re-pen-tance,
by the fall; If you tar-ry till you're bet-ter,
fond-ly dream; All the fit-ness He re-qui-reth

Full of pi-ty, love and pow'r.
Ev'-ry grace that brings you nigh.
You will ne-ver come at all. I will a-rise and
Is to feel your need of Him.

go to Je-sus, He will em-brace me in His arms;

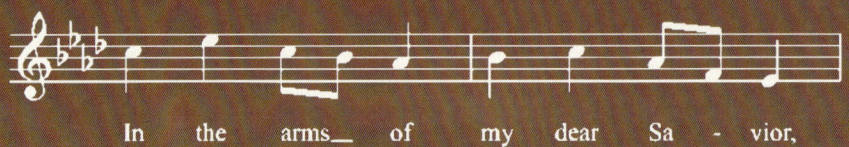

In the arms of my dear Sa-vior,

O there are ten thou-sand charms.

Read Matthew 11:28–30.

Reflect on this hymn and how it encourages or challenges you.

― Ways This Hymn Encourages Me ―

― Ways This Hymn Challenges Me ―

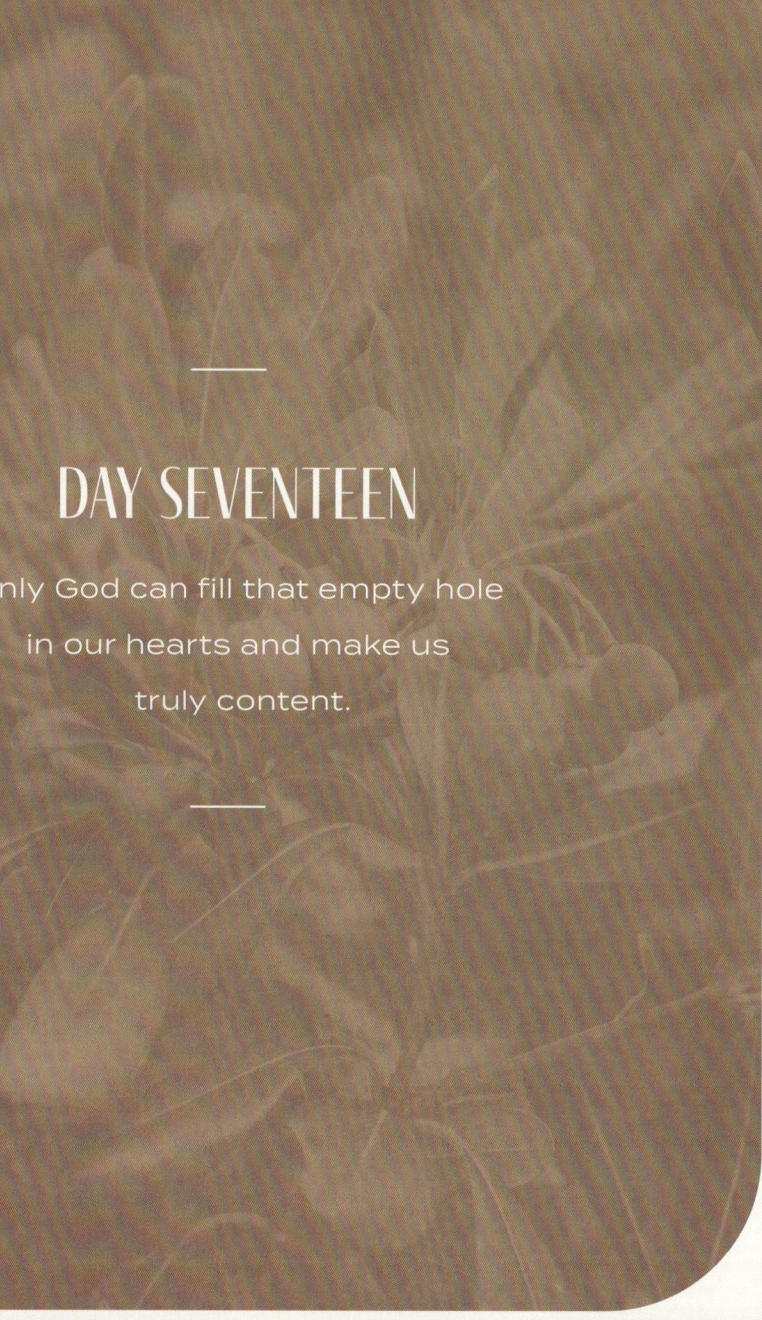

DAY SEVENTEEN

Only God can fill that empty hole in our hearts and make us truly content.

day seventeen

FORSAKING DISCONTENTMENT AND FINDING CONTENTMENT

Read Matthew 6:25–34, Philippians 4:10–13

Each one of us feels a sense of incompleteness at some point in our lives—like there is a hole in our hearts that needs to be filled. Even when life feels good and everything is going well, we can feel like something is missing, and until we have that thing, we will not be satisfied. These feelings often point us to the sin of discontentment. When we are discontent, we seek to place our hope and happiness in something else other than the Lord. But only God can fill that empty hole in our hearts and make us truly content.

The Sin of Discontentment

Our discontentment convinces us that something or someone other than God will make us happy. However, even if we obtain what we think will satisfy us, we often remain discontent. The hole in our hearts remains. Some of us try to push down this reality or keep trying to find things to fill our sense of emptiness. But the fact that nothing in this world can make us content points us to the truth that only God can satisfy us. Because God made us for Himself, He is our source of contentment. He is the One who gives us just what we need in His perfect timing.

From Death to Life

God knows what we need, and He will give us what we need because He is a faithful and loving Father. God's love for His children is deep, and He desires to pour out His blessings upon them. However, God will not always give us what we want. Though sometimes God does fulfill our desires, this is not a guarantee. Even so, we can still be content, knowing that even if we do not get what we want, God still loves us and gives us what we need in Himself.

While Matthew 6:25–34 mainly addresses anxiety, Jesus's words in this passage show us that we can fight discontentment by seeking the kingdom of God. When we seek God's kingdom, we will not be as focused on the things of this earth. Often, it is the things of this earth that make us discontent. For example, we grow discontent when we do not have the job, house, relationship, or appearance that we want. But when we shift our focus away from the kingdom of this earth to the kingdom of God, we are reminded that this world cannot satisfy us. We are reminded that even if we obtain what we want from this world, it will not provide us with lasting contentment.

Why? Because the things of this world were not meant to satisfy us. People may say that the things of this earth—such as money, fame, success, or possessions—make us happy. But the continuous discontentment people experience, even with those things, proves that the kingdom of this earth will never truly satisfy. Therefore, we are to seek God's kingdom first, trusting that God and His kingdom are all we need.

When we seek God's kingdom, we are able to be content no matter our current situations. Paul gives us an example of what this contentment looks like in Philippians 4:10–13. In this passage, Paul reveals how he has contentment regardless of whether he has much or little. Why? Because Paul's contentment is not rooted in his circumstances but in Christ. Therefore, the secret of being content is placing our contentment in Christ and not our circumstances.

How often do we base our contentment on our circumstances, though? Even though this is often our tendency, Paul shows us that we are able to place our contentment in Christ no matter our circumstances. Even when we experience lack, we can trust in the Lord. Even when we are suffering, we can remember that God is with us and helping us. Even when our prayers for something seem to go unanswered, we can praise the Lord for always being good.

Christ is enough because, in Christ, we have all that we need to be truly satisfied. In Christ, we receive true life, hope, and joy that cannot be removed from us even when we experience disappointments. How content we would be if we dwelt on these truths rather than on what we did not have! Because of Jesus, we are able to say every day and in every circumstance, "The Lord is my shepherd; I have what I need" (Psalm 23:1).

day seventeen reflection

What makes you discontent?

What does it look like for you to
place your contentment in Christ?

Read Psalm 23. How does this psalm
encourage your contentment in the Lord?

> The kingdom of this earth
> will never truly satisfy.
> Therefore, we are to seek
> God's kingdom first.

DAY EIGHTEEN

Jesus fulfills the connection we crave
and brings us into a family of believers
who give us a rich community.

day eighteen

FIGHTING LUST WITH CHRIST'S POWER

Read Psalm 16:11, Matthew 5:27–30

Yesterday, we discussed discontentment and how that sin connects to the sin of greed. And while our desire for something can lead to discontentment and greed, it can also lead to lust. In fact, sometimes the words "lust" and "greed" can be used synonymously. For example, someone may say that they lust after a certain item, job prospect, or relationship. But Scripture tends to typically link lust with sexual desire (Matthew 5:28). This might involve looking at another person and thinking impure thoughts about them or perhaps experiencing the desire for sex and going to pornography as an outlet for that lust. God's Word makes it clear that lust outside the covenant of marriage is sin. However, even though lust can be a struggle, we find hope for our struggle against lust in Jesus Christ.

The Sin of Lust

Often, lust is connected to deeper issues in our lives. The tendency to lust might be connected to the desire for affection. For example, we might so desperately desire another person's love that we allow ourselves to fantasize about a sexual connection in order to experience a sense of affection in our imagination. Lust might also be connected to loneliness or lack of general intimacy with other people. Therefore, we might turn to something like pornography, using it as an escape to satisfy our desires for connection.

In these instances, we rely on a certain media, act, or fantasy to give us something we feel is lacking, whether it be pleasure, affection, or connection. While we might believe that lust truly satisfies these desires, lust only perpetuates the problem. Instant gratification may physically give us what we want in the moment, but it cannot give us what we spiritually need.

From Death to Life

Our lustful desires are fought with the truth of the gospel. The gospel reminds us that we are given intimacy with the Lord through Christ, which is more powerful than physical intimacy. The gospel reminds us that while connection within an earthly relationship is sweet, Jesus fulfills the connection we crave and brings us into a family of believers who give us a rich community. And the gospel reminds us that sexual pleasure pales in comparison to the eternal satisfaction and joy we have in Christ. Our sinful flesh may convince us that seeking sexual fulfillment is what we need to be satisfied, but it is Jesus Christ alone who gives us true fulfillment and satisfaction.

What does this mean for our struggle with lust? It means that we can look to Christ to fulfill our every desire. Psalm 16:11 teaches us that it is God's presence that gives us true joy. It is the Lord who blesses us, not with fleeting pleasure but with eternal pleasures. Lust promises us security and satisfaction, but it will always fail to deliver the deep and permanent security and satisfaction Jesus provides. All of our desires that are connected to lust are met in Jesus Christ.

However, maybe there are times when lust feels too strong. We might know that we are to rest in Christ but still find ourselves struggling. What then? As believers, the new self we have in Christ releases us from the grip of sin. Therefore, though lust can be a difficult sin to conquer, it does not have to control us. Because of Christ, we have the ability and power to fight against lust. God's gift of the Holy Spirit enables us to exercise self-control in moments of temptation and gives us the ability to keep certain temptations and desires from turning into lust. The Spirit also helps us treat one another in the way God intended. In Christ, we are empowered to look at one another rightly, as brothers and sisters to love rather than objects to lust after.

> The new self we have in Christ releases us from the grip of sin.

Jesus gives us what we need to fight lust. He gives us His presence. He gives us eternal pleasures. He gives us true joy and satisfaction. May we praise Jesus for these blessings and rest in these blessings. Lust is strong, but God is stronger, and He will satisfy our every desire.

day eighteen reflection

Read 1 John 2:16–17. Why does lust not come from the Father? How does knowing that earthly pleasures are fleeting help you in your struggle with lust?

In what ways can you guard yourself against what induces lust?

Read and meditate on Philippians 4:8. Write out examples of what is true, honorable, pure, etc. Dwell on these things to keep your mind focused on Christ—on who He is and the extravagant love He has for you.

> "It is Jesus Christ alone who gives us true fulfillment and satisfaction."

DAY NINETEEN

When we meditate on
God's unchanging character,
we are able to move from
despair to hope.

day nineteen

GOING FROM HOPELESSNESS TO HOPEFULNESS

Read Lamentations 3:21–24, 1 Peter 1:3–4

Note: The following entry addresses the issue of despair. While we discuss it as a sin issue, we also recognize that there are medical reasons, such as clinical depression, for experiencing despair. Please note that any diagnosis of clinical depression must come from a medical professional who is qualified to diagnose and treat such physiological symptoms. You should never attempt to self-diagnose. If you think you may be struggling with clinical depression, please seek the help of a qualified mental health professional.

Things will never get better. I am going to feel this way forever. Nothing good will ever happen to me. These are thoughts of hopelessness and despair that can enter our minds in moments of pain and situations of suffering. It might surprise us to see hopelessness and despair listed as sins. But when we consider the hope believers have in Jesus Christ, we can understand how hopelessness and despair can be sins. When we are hopeless as believers, we are most likely not resting in the hope we have received through Christ. As believers, we have received a blessed hope, and we are to rest in this hope no matter what life brings.

The Sin of Hopelessness

We often struggle to have hope when we are put through troubling circumstances. When we experience a sudden diagnosis or health issue, we can be moved to despair. When a relationship falls apart or someone close to us passes, we can plunge into misery. When someone we love still refuses to give their life to Christ, we can lose hope that they will ever become a believer.

> Scripture gives a lifeline that keeps us from drowning in despair.

While it is okay to be sad and mourn in times of loss and brokenness, it is possible for us to plunge deep into despair. What is the difference between the two? Despair is different from sadness because it is a complete loss or absence of hope. When we keep our gaze on our troubles rather than on what is true, we find ourselves in this state of despair, allowing our grief to keep us from resting in the hope we have in Christ. In this choice not to place our hope in Him, we doubt what God can do and His ability to work through our circumstances for good. We make light of God's promises and sin against the One who loves us most. The biblical definition of hope is a joyful and confident expectation of our eternal salvation (Hebrews 11:1, 1 Peter 1:3–4). But when we do not have this expectation as believers, we essentially live as if there is no eternal salvation for us.

From Death to Life

The author of Lamentations teaches us that we can lament when we feel broken, grieved, and distressed while also choosing to place our hope in the Lord. The author of Lamentations is honest about his affliction and depression, but he follows up these words by declaring his hope in the Lord. His words show us what we can call to mind when we struggle to have hope. God is overflowing in faithful love. His mercies are new and never end. God's faithfulness is great. The Lord is our portion. When we meditate on God's unchanging character, we are able to move from despair to hope.

As believers, we can also meditate on the truths of the gospel when we feel low—the truth that Christ has given us a living hope that can never be taken away from us (1 Peter 1:3–4), the truth that nothing can separate us from the love of God in Christ (Romans 8:38–39), the truth that Jesus promises to return and make all things new (Revelation 21).

How can we remember and rest in these promises? By reading God's Word and meditating on its promises and truth. Scripture gives a lifeline that keeps us from drowning in despair. But yet, how often do we go to God's Word when we struggle to have hope? It is possible that we may move away from rather than toward Scripture in times of despair. Doing so only keeps our hearts from hearing the truth that we need to foster hope. No matter how hard our circumstances may be, God invites us to draw near to His Word and drink in the hope it provides.

> God invites us to draw near to His Word and drink in the hope it provides.

Though this world will bring suffering, we do not grieve as those without hope as believers (1 Thessalonians 4:13). While we can mourn the hard things of this life, let us not allow them to move us to despair. Even in the darkest times, our hope in Christ is a candle that will never burn out. The cares and troubles of life cannot extinguish our hope in Christ.

day nineteen reflection

What makes you hopeless or despair?

Why do we have true hope as believers?

Meditate on Romans 5:1–5.
What do these verses teach you about hope?

DAY TWENTY

As followers of Christ, our behavior should match the Savior we serve.

day twenty

TRADING HARSHNESS FOR GENTLENESS

Read Matthew 11:28–29, 1 Peter 3:3–4

When someone is harsh with us, it can feel like being inflicted with a wound. Their words or tone can be so sharp that it pierces our hearts and creates pain. Yet we inflict this same pain when we are harsh with others. While none of us would likely say that we enjoy it when people are harsh with us, we can sometimes forget how serious it is when we are harsh with others. As followers of Christ, our behavior should match the Savior we serve. We should not be harsh with others but gentle like Christ.

The Sin of Harshness

When we are harsh, we are cruel to someone; our words and tone are unpleasantly rough or sharp. While there is nothing wrong with communicating difficult things, speaking the truth, or even correcting others, we can do so with cruelty rather than love. Often, being harsh is connected to another sin. For example, we might be harsh to our kids because we are struggling to be patient with them. Or we might speak to our spouse in a biting tone because we are angry with them or responding out of our own selfishness. When we are harsh to another person, we exhibit an unloving attitude toward them. As we noted in the beginning, being harsh hurts others. And if harshness becomes consistently deliberate and persistent, it can even lead to abuse. The seriousness of harshness should cause us as believers to be careful with how we act, what we speak, and the way we say our words.

From Death to Life

Perhaps there are some of us who do not know how to overcome being harsh. Maybe we have tried hard to be patient, loving, and kind, but we still find ourselves being harsh with others. While this can be discouraging, we do not have to feel helpless in our desire to overcome harshness. As followers of Christ, we are empowered by the Spirit to be gentle.

The Bible shows us that believers are called, enabled, and empowered to act kindly. In fact, gentleness and kindness are fruit of the Spirit (Galatians 5:22–23). If gentleness and kindness are fruit of the Spirit, then we can exhibit these characteristics through the help of the Holy Spirit. But we also serve a Savior who is the very definition of gentleness. In Matthew 11:29, Jesus says that He is "lowly," which can also mean gentle. Paul affirms this truth in 2 Corinthians 10:1 by saying, "Now I, Paul, myself, appeal to you by the meekness and gentleness of Christ . . . "

Jesus's gentleness is displayed throughout the Gospels. Rather than rebuking those who brought little children to Him, Jesus welcomed the little children with open arms (Matthew 19:13–15). When an afflicted woman touched Jesus to receive healing, Jesus spoke lovingly to her (Luke 8:43–48). Jesus's gentleness shows us that there is another way to react than with harshness. There is a way for our words to be soothing rather than sharp. There is a way for our tone to be pleasing instead of painful. And this way is only possible through Jesus Christ by the power of the Spirit. As we rely on the Spirit, we are able to be gentle like our Savior is gentle. And in turn, others are pointed to Christ through our kind words and demeanor.

What would our responses to others look like if we depended more on the Spirit? How would our tone and words change if we allowed ourselves to slow down, pray, and ask the Spirit to help us speak kindly? We might find that we are not so quick to bite with our words. We might discover that our immediate response is more loving, gentle, and tender. This change in our words and behavior encourages our daily dependence on the Spirit.

God has enabled us to have a gentle heart and attitude through the Holy Spirit. So let us regularly rely on the Spirit to cultivate gentleness within us. Although our sinful nature can be quick to become harsh, we do not give in to our sinful nature. Through Christ and by the power of the Spirit, we can demonstrate the gentleness of Jesus in all of our words and actions.

> As followers of Christ, we are empowered by the Spirit to be gentle.

day twenty reflection

How are you prone to harshness?

Read 1 Peter 3:3–4. Why is a gentle and quiet spirit of great worth to God?

Write a prayer below, asking God to give you a gentle spirit like Christ.

> The Bible shows us that believers are called, enabled, and empowered to act kindly.

DAY TWENTY-ONE

We must keep our hearts
centered on Christ and rooted in the gospel.

day twenty-one

CHOOSING GRACIOUSNESS OVER GOSSIP

Read Psalm 141:3, Matthew 12:33–37

Gossip is like a small spark. It may seem harmless, but once ignited, it bursts into a flame and spreads like wildfire, consuming everything in its wake. It is no wonder that James 3:5–6 likens the tongue to fire. While we may write off gossip as minimal, gossip has the potential to create many problems and much pain. As believers, it is important that we keep from gossiping. Gossip does not reflect the character of Christ. Therefore, if we are to be Christlike in all of our ways as believers, we should be intentional, not just about our actions but also our words.

The Sin of Gossip

Gossip involves speaking and spreading information about someone behind their back. Some gossip can involve truthful information, while other gossip can be completely false. Often, gossip is rooted in our desire to please and be accepted by others. Therefore, we gossip as a way to earn the favor or acceptance of others. Gossip can also be rooted in a love of and thrill for drama. Many of us like spreading or hearing gossip—even if it does not ultimately matter to us or involve us—because we like to feel important or better about ourselves by gossiping.

If we are in Christ, we are to use our tongues to build up and not tear down (Ephesians 4:29). Yet there is no building up when it comes to gossip, only tearing down and breaking apart. We may believe that our gossip is harmless, but the spark of gossip bursts forth from a sinful heart. Jesus tells us in Matthew 12:34 that "the mouth speaks from the overflow of the heart." A good heart produces good things, such as good words. But a sinful heart produces evil, including evil words.

From Death to Life

As believers, we are able to speak good words because our hearts have been transformed by Christ. We have received Christ's righteousness as believers, and we are able to operate out of the righteousness we have in Christ through our words. However, sin can still sprout in our hearts, leading to gossip. This is why we must keep our hearts centered on Christ and rooted in the gospel. When we do, our words will reflect what is in our hearts. The good news of the gospel that we meditate on in our hearts will overflow out of us and produce words that build up others and please the Lord.

What does it look like to keep our hearts centered on Christ and rooted in the gospel? It looks like reading God's Word regularly. It looks like dwelling daily on the truth that Jesus loves us, died for us, and calls us to a new way of living. It might even look like choosing to pray when we feel tempted to gossip, asking Jesus to give us self-control. Perhaps our prayer could reflect the prayer of David in Psalm 141:3, which says, "Lord, set up a guard for my mouth; keep watch at the door of my lips." When we go to God in prayer and spend time in Scripture, our hearts are shaped by God's Word, allowing our words to reflect God's grace and truth.

What's more, by seeking to eliminate gossip, we set ourselves up to become trustworthy friends—and this is something we can only do through the power of the Spirit. One of the greatest ways we can be trustworthy friends is by loving people as Christ does. This involves choosing to keep confidential information to ourselves, even if sharing it would make us feel popular or well-liked. It involves valuing those around us and respecting their privacy. It involves being quick to pray for others rather than being quick to gossip about them.

What if we cared about showing Christ's love to others more than being accepted or affirmed by others? Gossip may be tempting, but with the help of the Lord, we can extinguish the spark of gossip. As believers, let us be known for speaking words that build up and bring life. Rather than spreading the wildfire of gossip, may the life-giving waters of the gospel flow from our lips, bringing grace to all who hear.

day twenty-one reflection

In what ways do you struggle with gossip?
What is your tendency to gossip rooted in?

What practical steps can you take to prevent gossip?

Pray Psalm 141:3 aloud slowly,
repeating or adding to the prayer if desired.

> As believers, let us be known for speaking words that build up and bring life.

DAY TWENTY-TWO

As followers of Christ, we are called to be humble in all that we say and do.

day twenty-two

PUTTING HUMILITY IN THE PLACE OF PRIDE

Read Psalm 115:1, Luke 18:9–14

Have you ever been in the presence of a prideful person? They likely made you feel uncomfortable or frustrated as they puffed up their chest, bragged about their accomplishments, or kept bringing the conversation back to themselves. It is not pleasant to be around a prideful person, but we may not realize that we can be prideful, as well. Pride is a sneaky sin because we do not always notice our prideful tendencies. Yet we can think thoughts and speak words of pride without realizing it. Though we may often fail to recognize our own pride, it is important that we be mindful of its tendency in our lives as believers. As followers of Christ, we are called to be humble in all that we say and do.

The Sin of Pride

Often, we can become prideful when we receive praise from others. While it is not wrong to appreciate praise, dwelling on praise and admiration from others can fuel our pride. Therefore, what we do with praise and admiration matters. If we allow someone's words to cause us to turn inward, we can easily boast about our own accomplishments and skills. And it is easy to turn inward as believers. Sin causes our good desire for ambition and excellence to become a selfish desire for affirmation and glory.

What's more, our sinful nature can convince us that we deserve to receive praise and admiration. After all, we are the ones with the prized trophies on the shelf, the certificates of accomplishment on the wall, or the impressive titles on the office door. But all of our skills, accomplishments, and accolades are gifts of grace. They are gifts given to us by a God who sovereignly orchestrated for us to receive them.

From Death to Life

Our hearts are humbled when we consider our sinful state. Each one of us is a sinner; we are all in need of mercy. There is nothing we can do to earn or deserve God's forgiveness and mercy. But in His grace, God sent us Jesus to give us mercy and forgive our sin. We continue to need God's mercy even after coming to faith in Christ. Our sinful flesh may tell us that we are able to be righteous in our own power, but we are not. We need God's grace in order to live obediently and righteously. In fact, we need God's grace to do anything of value. When we daily consider our sinfulness and need for God's mercy, we will be humbled.

The tax collector in Luke 18:9–14 exemplifies this attitude of humility. The Pharisee in this passage viewed himself as righteous and looked down upon those who were less righteous than him. In contrast, the tax collector exposed his sin to the Lord. He did not puff himself up before God but admitted his need for God's mercy. What if we postured ourselves like this tax collector? How much would our humility grow if we daily looked to God for mercy?

When we bow before the Lord and admit our utter helplessness (Psalm 115:1), we position ourselves to receive His mercy. And by His grace, God gives it to us. Because of Christ's forgiveness, we know that when we expose our sinfulness and helplessness to the Lord, we find grace and mercy (Hebrews 4:16). Therefore, as believers, the attitude we should possess is not a puffed-up chest but a humble heart.

> When we daily consider our sinfulness and need for God's mercy, we will be humbled.

Additionally, what if we daily meditated on God's greatness? God is the One who stands alone. He is above and before all things, and His power is vast and infinite. When we compare ourselves to the Lord, we are instantly humbled. We fall incredibly short of God's power and glory, and we should admit this truth rather than fight against it. The more we gaze upon God's glory, the less pride will fester in our hearts.

People in our world will continue to boast about themselves and seek glory, but we do not have to be like them as believers. Instead, we can live humbly by remembering the gospel and meditating on who God is, not seeking our own glory but giving all the glory to the Lord.

day twenty-two reflection

How do you struggle with pride?

How do the gospel and God's character humble you?

Reread Psalm 115:1. Write a prayer of praise to the Lord below, praising God for who He is and what He has done for you through Christ.

> "The more we gaze upon God's glory, the less pride will fester in our hearts."

Rock of Ages
Augustus Toplady

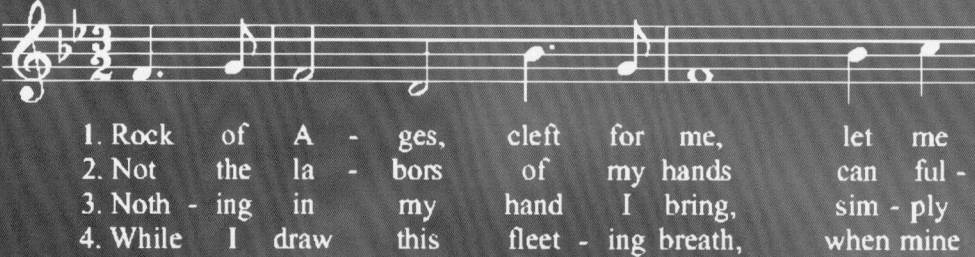

1. Rock of A - ges, cleft for me, let me
2. Not the la - bors of my hands can ful -
3. Noth - ing in my hand I bring, sim - ply
4. While I draw this fleet - ing breath, when mine

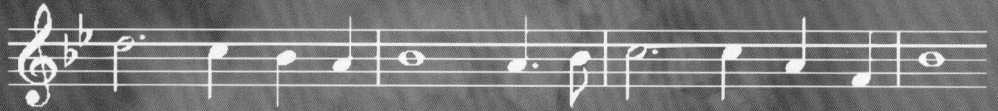

hide my - self in thee; let the wa - ter and the blood,
fill thy law's de - mands; could my zeal no re - spite know,
to the cross I cling; na - ked come to thee for dress;
eyes shall close in death, when I soar to worlds un known,

from thy woun - ded side which flowed, be of sin the
could my tears for - e - ver flow, all for sin could
help - less, look to thee for grace; foul, I to the
see thee on thy judg - ment throne, Rock of A - ges,

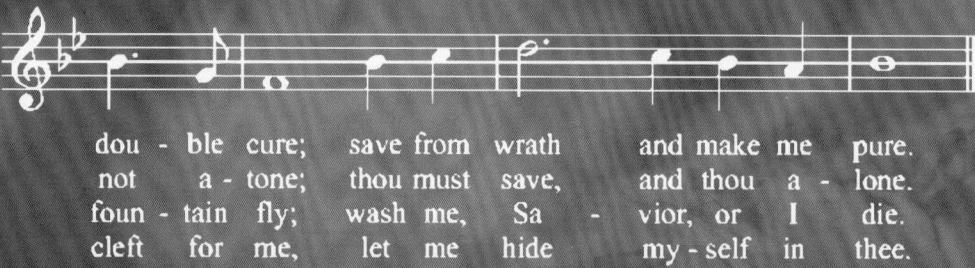

dou - ble cure; save from wrath and make me pure.
not a - tone; thou must save, and thou a - lone.
foun - tain fly; wash me, Sa - vior, or I die.
cleft for me, let me hide my - self in thee.

Read Psalm 62:1–2.

Reflect on this hymn and how it encourages or challenges you.

––––– Ways This Hymn Encourages Me –––––

––––– Ways This Hymn Challenges Me –––––

DAY TWENTY-THREE

Because everything belongs to the Lord,
all we have is a gift from God.

day twenty-three

TRADING SELFISHNESS FOR SELFLESSNESS

Read 1 Corinthians 10:24, Philippians 2:1–11

Generally, little kids are notorious for being unwilling to share. While some children may share easily or have moments when they are willing to share with others, most kids throw a fit when another kid takes their toy or wants what they have. They might either clutch what they have to themselves or scream loudly, "That's mine!" This reality reveals how our flesh thinks only of our own needs and our own happiness. We do not naturally want to give to others or think about others before ourselves, but these tendencies reveal the sin of selfishness that is the opposite of how Christ calls us to live.

The Sin of Selfishness

Selfishness causes us to think of ourselves alone. When we are selfish, we care only about what makes us the most happy and satisfied. And while it may feel good to be selfish because it gives us what we want, selfishness has consequences, causing "disorder and every evil practice" (James 3:16) and keeping us from loving others as we should. When we only focus on ourselves, the people around us are not cared for well—their needs are not met because we think only of our own needs.

A byproduct of selfishness is stinginess, which is similar to greed and is expressed when our love for what we have keeps us from giving it away. And stinginess is connected to selfishness as we can be closefisted over what we have, unwilling to share it with others. Stinginess is sinful because it causes us to believe that what we have is ours alone instead of the Lord's. Because everything belongs to the Lord, all we have is a gift from God—everything down to our last penny and possession. He is the One who provides for us, even if we are the ones doing the work to earn what we have.

After all, He is the One who gives us the opportunity and the ability to work in the first place. Therefore, our possessions are ultimately not ours to claim.

However, our sinful nature can cause us to say "mine" when it comes to what we have. We forget or dismiss the truth that everything belongs to the Lord, causing us to clutch our possessions tightly. An example of this can be found in the rich young ruler in Matthew 19:16–22. This man was willing to obey all the other commandments but unwilling to give up what he had. Even though Jesus told the man that he could have "treasure in heaven" (Matthew 19:21), the man clung to his treasures on earth. He was unwilling to make sacrifices in order to follow Jesus and receive eternal life in Him.

From Death to Life

Jesus reveals a different way of living through His sacrifice on the cross. By coming to earth as a servant and humbly dying in our place, Jesus showed Himself to be selfless rather than selfish. He did not focus on Himself but on us and our need for salvation. This selflessness and love led Him to die on the cross so that we could have salvation in Him. Jesus's sacrifice also shows us the opposite of stinginess. Jesus Christ is the ultimate example of a giver. Jesus willingly gave up His life for us on the cross in order to forgive our sins and grant us eternal life.

The gospel compels us to be selfless and generous people. Christ's generosity encourages us to willingly open our hands to give. Christ's sacrifice motivates us to consider others as more important than ourselves and look to the interests of others instead of to our own interests (Philippians 2:3–4, 1 Corinthians 10:24). The more we look to Christ, the more we will find our selfishness fade away and our desire to give increase.

The question we are to ask ourselves as believers is not "How can I serve myself?" but "How can I serve others?" It is not "How can I keep what I have?" but "How can I give more away?" These are the questions that posture our hearts to give and serve others. When we pray these words, asking God to show us how to give, we will reflect Christ's supreme generosity. We will reflect His sacrificial love. As we lay down our wants and desires for others, we will look increasingly like the One who gave everything for us.

> The gospel compels us to be selfless and generous people.

day twenty-three reflection

How do you struggle with selfishness?

How does the gospel compel you to be selfless?

Reread Philippians 2:1–11. Write a prayer below, asking the Lord to help you adopt the same attitude as Christ.

> Christ's generosity encourages us to willingly open our hands to give.

DAY TWENTY-FOUR

Followers of Christ are called to cultivate unity, not cause division.

day twenty-four

SEEKING UNITY OVER DIVISION

Read Ephesians 4:1–6, Philippians 2:2

Disagreement is something we all experience. Spouses can disagree over a decision regarding their kids' schooling. Students can disagree with other students about how they should go about doing a group project. Employees can disagree with a change their company leaders are seeking to implement. Disagreements can often be handled quickly, resolving the problem at hand. But sometimes, disagreements can be heightened, resulting in division.

When division occurs, a shift happens in structures and relationships. Something that was once whole breaks apart. Whatever it is that causes people to disagree results in those people setting themselves against each other or forfeiting the relationship altogether. We should be intentional as believers to not create and perpetuate division. Followers of Christ are called to cultivate unity, not cause division (Ephesians 4:1–6).

The Sin of Divisiveness

While it is possible for believers to graciously disagree with one another, sinful division happens when we purposely cause conflict with other people that leads to tension or a split in relationships. This division keeps believers from being united in the same mind and mission. The body of Christ is to be united in its heart and mission to spread the gospel, and we should not allow disagreements to threaten this mission. When believers allow conflict and disagreement to result in division, the body of Christ becomes stalled in its mission to spread the gospel. While God will continue to work within His Church whether there is division or not, the effectiveness of the body of Christ weakens when believers allow division to exist and fester.

From Death to Life

When we look at Jesus's ministry in the Gospels, we learn how Jesus treated all people with honor and respect. He was peaceable with all, and He never purposely caused division. As believers, we are enabled to be like our peaceful Savior through the help of the Spirit. Relying on the Spirit's power within us, we are empowered to treat all people, including our brothers and sisters in Christ, with love, honor, and respect. When we find that our response to others is causing conflict, the Spirit helps us seek forgiveness and pursue reconciliation with others.

Jesus enables us to be like Him, but He also unites us as God's people. The sacrifice of Christ unites us as believers and makes us one. What would it look like if we strived to maintain this gift of unity? What would the Church look like if each follower of Christ valued the unity Christ has given us? The more we cherish the unity Jesus has given us as believers, the less likely we are to allow division to occur.

Believers do not have to agree in all areas of life in order to have unity. But believers should agree on the gospel (Philippians 2:2). The body of Christ should have the gospel—the truth of Christ's salvation made possible through His death and resurrection—at its center. As believers, we are to have the same mindset by seeking to cherish and live out the gospel together. Therefore, we should be mindful of what is preventing the gospel from being at the center—not just in our churches but also in our lives. Are we allowing bitterness and jealousy to cause us to be divisive? Are we evaluating our own interests over the needs of others? Are we refusing to forgive others or fighting over small issues that are not actually important?

While it is important to pray for God's people to have unity, our actions matter as well. May we pray for unity while being mindful not to act in a way that is divisive. Let us desire for others to be harmonious while not being blind to our own divisive hearts. May our desire for God's people to be united start with us. As each member of the body of Christ strives for unity, the Church will flourish, lives will be changed, and God's name will be made known.

> The body of Christ is to be united in its heart and mission to spread the gospel.

day twenty-four reflection

How does the gospel encourage unity as believers?

In what ways can you pursue and maintain unity?

Meditate on Jesus's prayer from John 17:20–23. What does this prayer from Jesus reveal about God's desire for His people?

> As believers, we are enabled to be like our peaceful Savior through the help of the Spirit.

DAY TWENTY-FIVE

Even when we stumble or struggle with sin,
we remain loved and forgiven.

day twenty-five

EMBRACING HONESTY OVER HYPOCRISY

Read Proverbs 28:13, Matthew 23:27–28

Many movies contain the plot of someone in disguise. Whether they are a superhero, a spy, or a fugitive, these movie characters seek to hide their identity. But once they are in a safe and hidden place, their disguise comes off, and who they truly are is revealed. The sin of hypocrisy is similar to wearing a disguise. It involves a person presenting themselves as someone who they are not. Outwardly, they may say that they believe or follow some sort of practice, but in reality, they commit the opposite discreetly. And when they are found out, they are revealed for who they really are—a hypocrite.

The Sin of Hypocrisy

Hypocrisy always involves contradicting who you are or what you teach. Hypocrisy can also be connected to righteous behavior. For example, someone may go to church every Sunday and profess to be a Christian, but there is nothing about their life that reflects the faith they profess.

Jesus regularly called out hypocrites in the Gospels (Matthew 23:27–28). Jesus labeled the religious teachers of that day as hypocrites and revealed how these people honored God with their lips, but their hearts were actually far from Him (Mark 7:6–7). The Pharisees and scribes cared more about what they looked like on the outside and condemned others for not following the Law when they failed to do what the Law ultimately commanded—loving God and others.

We, too, can get caught up in having a righteous persona while hiding our sins from others. Our lives may seem obedient to God, but our hearts do not truly follow and worship God as they should. It can be discouraging to acknowledge that we can act hypocritically as believers, but acknowledging these tendencies is good. When our hypocrisy is brought to the surface, we are able to repent and ask God to help us live differently.

From Death to Life

We can still struggle with living honestly. We can fear being open and vulnerable in front of God and others because we are afraid we will be judged, rejected, or scorned. This is why the gospel is so important. The gospel reminds us of how Christ died for us, even though we sinned against Him. Jesus chose to die for us and give us salvation, even though He sees every one of our sins. When we place our faith in Jesus, we are given Christ's permanent grace and forgiveness. This means that even when we stumble or struggle with sin, we remain loved and forgiven.

> Christ's grace and forgiveness call us to come into the light and be seen.

Christ's grace and forgiveness call us to come into the light and be seen. His love and mercy beckon us to remove the mask and let ourselves be known. There is no reason to hide anything from God because we know we are given grace and mercy for every sin struggle (Proverbs 28:13). Our identity as forgiven sons and daughters motivates us to be honest with God. What's more, our identity in Christ motivates us to be honest with others. Knowing that we can bare everything to God because of Christ encourages us to be honest and open with others.

Again, we might still fear letting others see our sins and struggles. We might be afraid to confess our sins and shortcomings to others. While the devil desires for us to stay in the dark, Jesus invites us to become who He made us to be—children of the light through Him (Ephesians 5:8–14, 1 Thessalonians 5:5). Who we are in Christ motivates our honesty. The truth that we are loved, forgiven, and accepted—even though we sin—encourages us to be vulnerable with others. Imagine how our fears of being seen and known would dissipate if we daily rested and lived out our identity in Christ!

Because of Jesus, we do not have to hide. We do not have to look like someone we are not. As we seek to be faithful to Jesus while confessing our sins and shortcomings, we will live honestly and authentically as followers of Christ.

day twenty-five reflection

What are some ways Christians can struggle with hypocrisy?

How does the gospel encourage our honesty?

Write a prayer below, asking God to reveal any hypocrisy in your life and confess these areas to Him.

> The truth that we are loved, forgiven,
> and accepted — even though we sin —
> encourages us to be vulnerable with others.

DAY TWENTY-SIX

Instead of reacting impatiently,
we are able to react prayerfully
by coming to God for help.

day twenty-six

PURSUING PATIENCE OVER PRIDEFUL IMPATIENCE

Read Colossians 1:9–12, 2 Peter 3:9

A woman crosses her arms and taps her foot as she waits for the people in front of her to move through the grocery checkout. A man honks his horn and shakes his fist at the row of cars that are keeping him stuck in traffic. A parent yells at her kids to hurry up and put on their shoes because they are late. All of these instances involve impatience, and we might find one of these situations relatable for us. We all experience moments when our patience runs out, and we react impatiently. While these moments come easily, patience—rather than impatience—is to mark our lives as believers.

The Sin of Impatience

Like the above examples, impatience is usually reactionary. It causes us to become upset with others, either by getting angry with them or lashing out. It causes us to become anxious and irritable internally, and we can show this irritability in physical ways like tapping our fingers or letting out a groan. Impatience can also cause us to react negatively to God by feeling bitter against Him for not giving us what we want quickly.

Impatience is sinful—not only because it causes us to react sinfully but also because it is rooted in pride. When we grow impatient, it is often because we are not receiving what we want on our specific timetable. We want a quick drive to work, so we grow impatient with traffic. We want our kids to get out the door, so we become impatient with them. We might think, *I would be more of a patient person if everything worked out exactly when and how I wanted it to!* But unfortunately, that is not how life works. No matter how hard we try, we cannot control all of our circumstances all of the time. But this desire to control and to quickly satisfy our own wants can lead to a pattern of impatience.

From Death to Life

What if we allowed ourselves to slow down? How much would our lives look different if we did not rush from one thing to the next? Something that can help us slow down is considering our eternity. If we are in Christ, we have a future home with the Lord. We are often so focused on the present and what is occupying the here and now. But consider the change that could come if we lifted our eyes and looked toward eternity. Eternity with the Lord is ahead of us as believers, which means that we can see our temporal time in the present as something to lean into for God's glory rather than control for our own. When we see every day, hour, and minute as a gift God gives us to serve and honor Him, we will go about our lives with intentionality and joy rather than impatience and stress. And doing so allows us to humbly accept God's plans and purposes for our lives rather than trying to seize control for ourselves.

Scripture teaches us that God is the epitome of patience (2 Peter 3:9). And because God is patient, His people are able to be patient. Those who come to faith in Christ are able to be like the patient God they serve through the power of the Spirit. But do we come to God for patience? Do we ask God to give us patience and help us in the moments we feel impatient? Often, we allow ourselves to remain in that place of impatience, or we simply try to get past it on our own. Yet God is willing to give us His strength and patience (Colossians 1:11). Instead of reacting impatiently, we are able to react prayerfully by coming to God for help. Going to the Lord also helps us with the root of our impatience—pride. Because of Christ, we can come before the Lord and ask Him to humble our hearts.

The patience God supplies us with helps us to be patient with Him and others. When we remember God's patience, we will be encouraged to exhibit patience through His strength. And we will be able to wait with patience no matter the season or circumstance.

> Because of Christ, we can come before the Lord and ask Him to humble our hearts.

day twenty-six reflection

How do you struggle with impatience?

What is often at the root of your impatience?

Write a plan below for how you want to rely on the Lord
in the moments when you feel impatient.

> When we remember God's patience, we will be encouraged to exhibit patience through His strength.

DAY TWENTY-SEVEN

We are to respond to God's mercy by showing mercy toward others through forgiveness.

day twenty-seven

EXTENDING FORGIVENESS INSTEAD OF UNFORGIVENESS

Read Matthew 18:21–35, Mark 11:25

Note: While this text addresses forgiveness, for situations of abuse, neglect, or relational trauma, the path to forgiveness may be a long and uphill climb—and forgiveness may not always result in the restoration of some relationships on this side of eternity. As you wrestle with forgiving those who have wronged you, seek support from your local church or from a trusted counselor. In Christ, we are set free from bitterness, anger, and shame. He will bring healing for every hurt. And one day, Christ will make all things right again.

A little girl comes into her parents' room with tears streaming down her face. "What is wrong?" her mother asks her. Between sobs and hiccups, the girl confesses that she accidentally broke her mom's vase as she was running down the hall. "I am so sorry," the little girl says. "Will you forgive me?" The mother wraps her child up in her arms and says to her, "Of course I forgive you." This situation is a sweet picture of forgiveness.

However, this kind of forgiveness can be harder when it comes to adult relationships and situations. Forgiveness comes easier when the offense is small, but if the offense is great, forgiveness can seem impossible. When we choose not to forgive, we might somehow think that we are saving ourselves from trouble and pain. But unforgiveness only perpetuates anger, bitterness, and resentment toward the person who has hurt us or sinned against us.

The Sin of Unforgiveness

Unforgiveness in our lives can look like bringing up the wrong someone has done against us, even if they have asked for forgiveness. It can look like remaining bitter or angry at another person because of something they did to us. Scripture gives us a picture of unforgiveness in the parable of the unforgiving servant (Matthew 18:21–35). In this parable, a servant owes a king a substantial amount of money. When he pleads with the king to give him more time to acquire the money, the king has compassion on the servant and chooses to forgive the servant's debt. However, instead of responding humbly, that servant then finds another servant and demands that he give him the money that is owed to him. After the second servant cries a similar plea, the first servant refuses to forgive his debt. When the king hears about what the first servant has done, he tells him, "Shouldn't you also have had mercy on your fellow servant, as I had mercy on you?" (Matthew 18:33).

> Dwelling on Christ's forgiveness for us moves us to forgive others.

From Death to Life

The king's mercy was meant to teach the servant to be merciful himself. In the same way, we are to respond to God's mercy by showing mercy toward others through forgiveness. Specifically, Colossians 3:13 tells us that we are to forgive others because God has forgiven us. Though we did not deserve such grace, Jesus died for us. Through His sacrifice, Jesus forgives us of our sins and clears the debt we owe to God for our sin. Jesus is our compassionate and gracious King who has forgiven our debt by His own blood. As believers, we are to respond to such forgiveness by forgiving others.

We may know these truths as believers, but it can still feel too hard and perhaps even impossible to forgive. *If you only knew how much this person hurt me, you would not expect me to forgive*, we may say to Jesus. However, how would remembering the forgiveness you have received impact how you forgive others? Dwelling on Christ's forgiveness for us moves us to forgive others. When we meditate on the gospel, we are reminded of how Christ has forgiven us and keeps forgiving us, even though our offense against Him was great. Jesus freely died to forgive our sin, calling us to respond with faith and repentance. Therefore, we are to forgive others even when people do not deserve our forgiveness. We are to forgive even when the person's offense against us seems insurmountable. We are to forgive with no conditions attached.

And in the moments we struggle to forgive, we can remember Christ's understanding and empathy. Jesus knows what it is like to forgive while also experiencing the pain that comes from others' sin (Luke 23). Jesus sees our tears. He feels our hurt. He understands the struggle. We can come to Christ when it feels painful to forgive, knowing that He empathizes with us and gives us the strength to forgive. And we can entrust justice to Christ in all circumstances, knowing that Jesus will judge the sins that are committed against us.

So let us ensure that we are walking in forgiveness as believers. Let us not withhold forgiveness from others but grant it freely, even when it hurts. In light of Christ's great forgiveness toward us, may we be forgiving toward others.

> In light of Christ's great forgiveness toward us, may we be forgiving toward others.

day twenty-seven reflection

In what ways do you struggle with forgiveness?

How does Christ's forgiveness encourage you to forgive?

Is there anyone in your life you need to forgive?
Write a prayer below, asking Jesus to help you forgive.
Additionally, consider taking the next step
and telling that person you forgive them.

DAY TWENTY-EIGHT

Gradually, anger will start to
lose its grip on us as we
delight in His grace
and walk by the Spirit.

day twenty-eight

REPLACING SINFUL ANGER WITH CHRIST'S RIGHTEOUSNESS

Read Matthew 5:21–24, James 1:19–20

If you have ever watched a cartoon before, you know what it looks like to watch a character become angry. Their face turns red, their fists clench, and steam shoots out of their ears. While it can be comical to watch this character react, we know that we also react similarly sometimes. We all experience anger, and each of us responds differently when we are angry. However, sometimes we can make excuses for our anger, especially in light of the situation at hand. For example, if someone sideswipes our car on the highway, we might feel that it is justified to be angry. Even still, anger can be a sin, and we should be careful as believers not to give in to the anger that arises.

The Sin of Unrighteous Anger

Unrighteous anger is anger that stems from a sinful motivation or has a sinful response. We should take unrighteous anger seriously as believers. Matthew 5:21–22 teaches us that anger with another can be just as serious as murder and have serious consequences. Anger harms our relationships and will be judged by God. James 1:20 also tells us that "human anger does not accomplish God's righteousness." This means that unrighteous anger does not produce righteous actions. Nothing good and godly comes from this kind of anger. Therefore, when we are unrighteously angry as believers, we fail to practice the righteousness we have been given through Christ.

As we have discussed, living as believers involves actions such as love, patience, kindness, and humility. Anger is the opposite of these actions. When we are angry, we can be unkind to others and say things that hurt them. We can treat people in a way that is not loving and make people feel insecure or invaluable.

From Death to Life

On the cross, Jesus took on our unrighteousness so that we could be made righteous. When we put our faith in Him, we are cleansed from our unrighteousness and given His righteousness (2 Corinthians 5:21). Because of Christ's righteousness, we are now innocent and holy in the eyes of God. And with Christ's righteousness, we are transformed to be able to be like Christ. We still may struggle with sinful anger, but we do not struggle without hope for change. In the moments when we are tempted toward sinful anger, we can remember the extravagant patience of God in Christ. We can reflect on Christ's compassion for us. Christ's death on the cross means that God's wrath and anger are no longer directed toward us — so what cause do we have to be wrathful or sinfully angry with others?

As we remember the grace of Christ, we will naturally become increasingly encouraged to share this grace with others. Gradually, anger will start to lose its grip on us as we delight in His grace and walk by the Spirit.

Yet, even still, there may be some of us who feel like we keep failing in this area. Perhaps we try so hard to be slow to anger but still find ourselves erupting. Controlling our anger is certainly difficult, but it is not impossible. As we daily depend on the Spirit and ask Jesus to change our hearts and our responses, we will find our anger dissipating. Growing in our sanctification in this area can be tough, but it can be encouraging to know that God helps us control our anger as He shapes us more into the image of His Son.

What would it look like, then, to depend on the Lord to help us control our anger? What could we do in the moments when we find anger bubbling up? Perhaps we could take a deep breath and slow ourselves down. Perhaps we could take a step away to pray. We might even pause the conversation and pray with the person who is making us upset. Or we could ask the Spirit to show us what is at the root of our anger and help us conquer that issue.

As we depend on the Spirit daily, we will also learn to have righteous anger. Righteous anger is what we see demonstrated by God in response to sin. For instance, Jesus responded with righteous anger when He saw the hard hearts of the Pharisees (Mark 3:5). This kind of anger is not sinful because it is a good and just reaction to sin. Sin should grieve us, and we should be angered by the sin that goes on around us.

While anger can be hard to control or overcome, we are able to respond differently to conflict or stress with the help of the Spirit. So let us aim to accomplish the righteousness of God in our lives by walking in love, patience, and forgiveness. Sinful anger has no place in our hearts when we are living as God commands.

day twenty-eight reflection

How do you struggle with anger?

What is often at the root of your anger?

Journal some thoughts below regarding what it could look like for you to turn to the Lord and rely on the Spirit whenever you feel angry.

> God helps us control our anger as He shapes us more into the image of His Son.

Read Hebrews 9:11–14.

Reflect on this hymn and how it encourages or challenges you.

───── **Ways This Hymn Encourages Me** ─────

───── **Ways This Hymn Challenges Me** ─────

DAY TWENTY-NINE

Instead of judging others, we are to evaluate ourselves and confess our own blindspots and sin issues.

day twenty-nine

BEING KIND INSTEAD OF JUDGMENTAL

Read Matthew 7:1–5

A group of friends is waiting at a crosswalk, eager to go across the road and get to the restaurant where they have reservations. While they stand there, they are approached by a man in battered and dirty clothes. "Please, do you have any money you could spare?" the man asks the group of friends. Immediately, the friends make a face and turn away from him. "He will just spend the money on alcohol," one of the friends whispers. "It's his fault for allowing himself to get in this place," another friend says as the crosswalk changes, and they begin to walk. "I know. I would never let myself sink that low," another friend responds.

The Sin of Judgment

The above scenario is an example of being judgmental. These friends criticized the poor man and made assumptions about him because of his situation. We might read the previous scenario and think, *I would never do that*. But even if we do not speak similar words, we often think similar thoughts in our minds. For example, we might look at what someone is wearing and make a quick judgment about them based on their outfit. Or we might notice someone's behavior in public and assume something negative about their intentions. When we are judgmental, we essentially pass a negative verdict on someone in a critical or condemning manner. Judging others in this way does not show the love of Christ.

Often, sinful judgment is rooted in pride. When we criticize or condemn someone, we often do so to feel better about ourselves. Our judgment could even cause us to believe that we are better than someone else. We might think, *At least I do not act or look like that*. Judging others can also be connected with gossip. Our gossip might involve judging someone with other people. We should evaluate ourselves to see if these tendencies are evident in our lives and be quick to repent of them.

From Death to Life

Jesus teaches us that we must evaluate ourselves before we even think about evaluating others. When we judge others, we often forget that there is sin in our lives that deserves judgment. Instead of judging others, we are to evaluate ourselves and confess our own blindspots and sin issues. Jesus's use of the words "splinter" and "beam" in Matthew 7:4 reminds us that our own sin is grave and needs to be taken seriously. Even if someone else's sin issue seems to be "greater" than our own, our sin is still big in the eyes of God, and therefore, it should be treated seriously.

> The more we humble ourselves, the more we will be gracious in our thoughts, words, and actions.

Taking the time to evaluate the "beam" in our own eyes is an act of humility. And humility is what keeps us from sinfully judging others. As believers, when we consider how we are sinful and yet so unconditionally loved by God, we are humbled. When we realize how God looks favorably upon us because of Christ, we are humbled to look favorably upon others. And when we remember that God does not condemn us because of Christ's forgiveness, we are encouraged not to condemn others (Romans 8:1). Christ's salvation has saved us from God's judgment, and it is in light of His great grace and mercy that we are to be people of grace and mercy.

How would daily humbling ourselves shape how we see others? We might find ourselves thinking lovingly rather than critically about other people. We might see that we are quick to repent when we experience a judgmental thought. We might find ourselves eager to pray for those we immediately judge. Or perhaps we find ourselves moved to show grace and mercy to those who are lost or hurting. The more we humble ourselves, the more we will be gracious in our thoughts, words, and actions.

Even if someone is doing something wrong, we can still think and speak about them in a way that is loving and kind. In doing so, we reflect our God, who loves us and gives us His grace even when we sin. As God's people, may we not be known for being people of judgment but people of grace who seek to look at and think about others just as God does.

day twenty-nine reflection

In what ways do you struggle with judging others?

What is at the root of your judgment?

Write a prayer below, asking God to help you see and treat others with grace and mercy rather than judgment.

> As God's people, may we not be known
> for being people of judgment
> but people of grace.

DAY THIRTY

The gospel humbles us and reminds us that we have been given every spiritual blessing in Christ.

day thirty

FIGHTING BITTERNESS WITH GOD'S FAITHFULNESS

Read Ephesians 4:31, Philippians 4:19–20

When we eat or drink something that is bitter to the taste, it is usually not pleasant. The bitter food or drink we consume typically makes us turn up our faces in disgust. When we become bitter, our reactions can be similar. That feeling of bitterness is not enjoyable, and it usually leads to a sour and displeased reaction. Often, we experience bitterness in response to a situation we face or in response to something that someone else has that we lack. Though life's circumstances can leave us bitter, it is sinful to respond in this way. Scripture calls us to put away bitterness and shows us how we can fight bitterness by trusting the Lord (Ephesians 4:31).

The Sin of Bitterness

Bitterness usually occurs when we compare ourselves to others. We scroll on social media and see someone experiencing a beautiful vacation when we have not taken a trip in years. So we grow bitter. We receive news that a friend is pregnant when we have been trying to get pregnant for far longer. So we grow bitter. Someone at work is chosen for the new promotion that we wanted. So we grow bitter.

Bitterness can also occur when we become upset with God over what He is doing. If we are in a season of waiting or suffering, we can accuse God of being cruel or treating us unfairly. Naomi's story in the book of Ruth gives us an example of this type of bitterness. When Naomi's two sons and husband died, Naomi was left childless and a widow. Even though one of her daughters-in-law, Ruth, decided to stay with her as she returned home, she told those she knew, "Don't call me Naomi. Call me Mara . . . for the Almighty has made me very bitter. I went away full, but the LORD has brought me back empty. Why do you call me Naomi, since the LORD has opposed me, and the Almighty has afflicted me?" (Ruth 1:20–21). While the name Naomi means "pleasant," the name Mara means "bitter." Thus, this name change demonstrates how Naomi viewed her difficult circumstances. She believed that God had set Himself against her by bringing this suffering upon her, and that made her bitter.

From Death to Life

Yet God proved His faithfulness to Naomi. He led her daughter-in-law Ruth to a man named Boaz. Ruth and Boaz married, and because Boaz was related to Naomi, He redeemed Naomi's land and gave her the security she needed. Ruth also gave birth to a son, providing Naomi with the joy of being a grandmother. Scripture shows us how Naomi's grandson went on to become the grandfather of the future king of Israel—David (Ruth 4:17). Such blessings reveal that God had not forgotten Naomi or abandoned her. Naomi's story reminds us that we can still see God's goodness even if our circumstances are bad. God is always working in our lives and blessing us, even if we cannot see it or understand what He is doing (Philippians 4:19–20).

While Naomi's story may encourage us, we might still find bitterness in our hearts. This is where the gospel comes in. The gospel humbles us and reminds us that we have been given every spiritual blessing in Christ (Ephesians 1:3). In Christ, we have received salvation and eternal life. Therefore, we do not have to be bitter when someone else has something we lack because we have exactly what we need in Christ. How our bitterness would shift if we regularly dwelt on Christ's blessings!

> When we stop and consider God's faithfulness in the past, present, and future, we will be kept from becoming bitter.

Remembering what God has done, is doing, and will do also helps us in our bitterness. What if we looked back and saw how God gave us His Son to save us? What if we looked to the present and found ways that God is blessing us and growing us? What if we looked to the future and rested in the eternity we have in Christ? When we stop and consider God's faithfulness in the past, present, and future, we will be kept from becoming bitter over what we lack or the hard situations we experience. So let us remember that God has been and will always be good to us. God's faithfulness and goodness wash away our bitterness and replace it with joy and gratitude.

day thirty reflection

How are you prone to bitterness?

What is at the root of your bitterness?

List three to five ways God has been faithful to you below.

> "God's faithfulness and goodness wash away our bitterness and replace it with joy and gratitude."

DAY THIRTY-ONE

When we daily worship the Lord
with our lips and lives,
we are humbled.

day thirty-one

RESISTING JEALOUSY BY RESTING IN CHRIST

Read Luke 15:25–32, James 3:14–18

Have you ever heard someone refer to a "green-eyed monster"? This term is used to personify jealousy. And if we look at our own lives and our hearts, we might likely see how jealousy can make us monstrous. When we are jealous, our bitterness and anger can make us snarl inwardly and want to attack the person making us jealous. This reaction reveals how jealousy is sinful. While it can be easy to give in to jealousy, we fail to love others as we should when we are jealous as believers.

The Sin of Jealousy

Jealousy is similar to coveting in that it causes us to desire something really badly—usually something that someone else has. For example, we might become jealous of a friend who is in a relationship when we are single. Or we might grow jealous of a family member who seems to receive more attention than us. The brother in the parable of the prodigal son exhibited this type of jealousy (Luke 15:28–30). When the prodigal son received a celebration, even though he had left home and squandered his father's money, his brother became bitter and jealous.

Jealousy is often rooted in pride, insecurity, and discontentment. Jealousy is rooted in pride when we believe that we deserve or are owed what someone else has. Jealousy is rooted in insecurity when we believe we need something in order to make ourselves feel loved, secure, or seen. And jealousy is rooted in discontentment when we allow our desire for something to move us to bitterness rather than trusting in the Lord's provision. Alternatively, we may not grow bitter but instead come to idolize the part of our lives over which we are discontent.

Jealousy is dangerous because it can harm our relationships with others. We might lash out at someone we are jealous of, or we might allow our jealousy to cause us to separate from those we are jealous of. None of these responses lead to healthy relationships. In fact, James 3:16 says that envy, or jealousy, results in "disorder and every evil practice." Jealousy does not bring order but disorder. It creates division and ruins relationships rather than creating and building up healthy relationships.

From Death to Life

The father's response to the jealous brother in the parable of the prodigal son teaches us valuable truth. The brother did not need to be bitter and angry because the father had already given the brother everything (Luke 15:31). Similarly, we can fight jealousy by meditating on what we have in Christ. Meditating on what we have in Christ keeps us from seeking anything apart from Christ to make us feel happy or secure. When someone receives something we do not have, we are able to rest in what we do have in Christ. And what we do have in Christ far surpasses any earthly or material gain. What do we have in Christ? We have an eternal home. We have a peace that is beyond our understanding. We have a hope that cannot die.

We also have an identity in Christ. We are loved despite our struggles, chosen despite our failures, adopted despite our rebellion, and forgiven despite our sins. When we rest in our identity in Christ, we will not allow what someone else has or receives to threaten our identity. We will not seek to find our identity in any relationship, job, or possession. Consider how content we would be if we regularly rested in our identity in Christ.

And if we find our jealousy is connected with pride, how might our worship change our hearts? When we daily worship the Lord with our lips and lives, we are humbled. We are reminded that God is the One who is great and deserves all the glory. This truth helps us confess that our lives are not about ourselves but about God. Therefore, when we set our gaze on the Lord instead of on ourselves, we are able to react with humility rather than jealousy when someone receives something we do not have.

So as followers of Christ, let us not allow the green-eyed monster to rear its ugly head. Let us rest in who we are in Christ and what we have in Christ as we seek to live as the loving, humble people God has created us to be.

day thirty-one reflection

How are you prone to jealousy? What causes your jealousy?

List below at least three things you have in Christ that you can rest in when you feel jealousy creeping into your heart.

Write a prayer to God, asking Him to reveal areas where you have grown jealous. Repent of your jealousy, and ask Him to help you rest in Christ.

"

For where there is envy and selfish ambition,
there is disorder and every evil practice.

JAMES 3:16

"

DAY THIRTY-TWO

Followers of Christ are to be like shining stars that point to the One who is light and life.

day thirty-two

CHOOSING GRATITUDE OVER GRUMBLING

Read Exodus 16:1–3, Psalm 100:4–5

"Are we there yet?" a little kid asks with an exasperated sigh. "I do not want to do this!" says a teenager as he takes out the trash. "This is just so annoying," a young woman says to her friend on the phone. All of these are examples of grumbling, or complaining, and we might find that we have uttered the same or similar words ourselves. Complaining comes pretty naturally to our sinful flesh. When we become frustrated or annoyed, we are likely to complain. When something inconveniences us or when things do not go our way, we are likely to complain. And while we might write these complaints off or try to justify them, our complaining reveals the sinful tendencies of pride and distrust in God.

The Sin of Grumbling

Complaining is always centered around our needs, wants, and desires not being met. It is similar to discontentment but differs in the fact that complaining typically has an audible reaction. When we complain, we often do so with noises of dissatisfaction, a tone of annoyance, and words that express the frustration we feel in our hearts. We see an example of this type of reaction in the wilderness narratives. The Israelites complained to God many times when they were in the wilderness, and their complaining almost always focused on their physical needs not being met (Exodus 15:23–24). Like the Israelites, our complaining is often about what we think is hindering our needs and wants. And our complaining often reveals a lack of trust in who God is and His good plans. In our complaints, we essentially say to God, "I do not trust You, You are not enough, and You are not being fair."

When we complain, we fail to acknowledge the ways in which God has been good to us in the past. We look at our current circumstances or specific sufferings and complain that God does not have our best interests at heart. We accuse Him of giving us this hard situation while forgetting that He has brought us through similar circumstances and has done so for our good. The Israelites did this by grumbling against God even though He had just released them from the horrors of slavery (Exodus 16:1–3).

From Death to Life

Paul tells us in Philippians 2:14–15, "Do everything without grumbling and arguing, so that you may be blameless and pure, children of God who are faultless in a crooked and perverted generation, among whom you shine like stars in the world." Followers of Christ are to be like shining stars that point to the One who is light and life. And we live like shining stars by refraining from grumbling.

However, actually doing everything without grumbling is difficult, especially when life is really hard. This is why the practice of lament can help us. Lament involves bringing our feelings and frustration to God in prayer. David shows us what it looks like to lament in Psalm 142:1–2 by saying, "I cry aloud to the Lord; I plead aloud to the Lord for mercy. I pour out my complaint before him; I reveal my trouble to him." David shows us in these verses that there is a godly form of complaint.

This is called lament, and it is an honest cry to God that expresses what we are going through and asks for God's help. How might we feel and react differently if we chose this godly type of complaining?

Consider how a consistent heart of gratitude can also keep us from complaining. When we thank the Lord, our eyes are fixed on Him and not ourselves. When we lean into the work of the Spirit within us, our hearts are moved to gratitude as the Spirit sanctifies us through our obedience. Praising God for who He is and what He does reminds us that God is good no matter our circumstances (Psalm 100:4–5). And when we are inconvenienced or when we experience suffering, gratitude allows us to thank God for how He is working, even if we do not understand what He is doing. While it can be easy to complain, we do not have to give in to this tendency as believers. With God's help, we are able to put away grumbling by choosing gratitude.

> Gratitude allows us to thank God for how He is working, even if we do not understand what He is doing.

day thirty-two reflection

What causes you to complain? How can you practice lament when you are in a troubling or vexing situation?

How does grumbling keep us from being "shining stars"?
(See Philippians 2:14–15.)

List three to five things below that you are grateful for, and then spend some time in prayer, thanking God for these things.

> "With God's help, we are able to put away grumbling by choosing gratitude."

DAY THIRTY-THREE

Christ's salvation has changed us,
enabling us to live differently
than who we once were.

day thirty-three

LOVING TRUTH OVER LIES

Read Ephesians 4:25

A shattering noise comes from the other room, and a mother goes to see what caused the noise. Her two young sons stand in the living room, where they are surrounded by shattered pieces on the floor. "Who broke this lamp?" the mother asks her children. "He did it!" each of the boys say as they point at one another. It is clear that one of her sons is lying.

Lying is common for many children because children do not like to get in trouble. They want to avoid potential discipline, so they would rather lie in order to try and keep themselves safe from punishment. As adults, we do not usually struggle with lying like kids do—at least, not in the same way. While some of us do lie out of fear of punishment, many of us lie out of fear of man. We might lie to receive attention or approval. We might stretch the truth about what we do or about our past so that we seem appealing to others. Or we may lie to avoid hard conversations with others. We might withhold the truth so that we do not stir up any complications in our relationships. However, lying is sinful, no matter the ways in which we lie. And when we lie, we do not live as the lovers of truth that God calls us to be.

The Sin of Lying

Lying harms our relationships with others. Telling the truth is right and beneficial, but withholding the truth delays or destroys growth and trust. Honesty builds others up and keeps us unified. But lying only hurts harmony and causes division and disunity. Lying is also in direct contrast with our new selves. Paul writes in Colossians 3:9–10a, "Do not lie to one another, since you have put off the old self with its practices and have put on the new self." This verse teaches us that lying is associated with our old selves. As we have noted, God created us to reflect His truthfulness. Therefore, our new selves are to look and act differently than our old selves by their fidelity to the truth.

From Death to Life

If lying was part of who we once were without Christ, it should not be evident in our lives now that we are in Christ (Ephesians 4:25). Knowing that lying is part of the old self encourages us because we know that our new selves are capable of being honest. Christ's salvation has changed us, enabling us to live differently than who we once were. Such truth motivates us to take on the new self with joy and live honestly. But if we find ourselves being like our old selves by lying, we can remember that if we are in Christ, we are forgiven. We do not have to hide anything from God because we have been forgiven in Christ. Therefore, we can be honest with God, even about our sin. And if we can be honest with God, we can be honest with others, too.

But what about the deeper issues that keep us from being truthful? We have the Spirit in us who helps us fight against sinful tendencies that lead to lying. If we struggle with the fear of man, the Spirit helps us to fear the Lord above all. The more we fear the Lord—by worshiping Him and delighting in who He is—the less we will focus on pleasing man. In response to our fear of the Lord, we will be honest with others rather than lying to look a certain way or impress others. We will care more about being faithful in the eyes of God than popular in the eyes of man.

The Spirit also reminds us of who we are in Christ. If we are rejected for being truthful, we are still accepted because of Christ. If we lose a relationship because of our honesty, our relationship with Christ remains secure. Why should we fear others' responses to our truthfulness if who we are in Christ and what we have in Christ remain? The Spirit helps us to be people of truth, so let us rely on Him to speak truthfully. May our relationship with Christ encourage us to be lovers of the truth.

> We do not have to hide anything from God because we have been forgiven in Christ.

day thirty-three reflection

In what ways do you struggle with lying?

Read John 8:44 and Numbers 23:19.
What do these verses say about who God is compared to Satan?
How can you reflect who God is through your speech?

Meditate on Ephesians 4:15 and write below any thoughts you may have on what speaking the truth in love could look like.

> "The Spirit helps us to be people of truth,
> so let us rely on Him to speak truthfully."

DAY THIRTY-FOUR

What leaves our mouths reveals the condition of our hearts.

day thirty-four

SPEAKING GRACIOUSLY INSTEAD OF OBSCENELY

Read Luke 6:45, Ephesians 4:29

Most parents teach their children that there are certain words they should not say. Parents typically tell their children that these are "bad words," and some parents warn their kids that they will be punished if they say these words. Perhaps some of us even know what it is like to get our mouths washed out with soap for saying bad words as children. When we get older, however, we all have a choice to make over whether we will say these kinds of words or not. But as believers, we are specifically challenged by Scripture to not only refrain from speaking bad words but to refrain from any kind of obscene talk.

The Sin of Obscene Talk

The Bible says that obscene talk is anything that involves "foul language" (Ephesians 4:29), "filthy language" (Colossians 3:8), or "obscene and foolish talking or crude joking" (Ephesians 5:4). In Ephesians 4:29, the Greek word for "foul" essentially means "rotten." Consider a rotting fruit. Rotten fruit is detestable, and it is prone to make any fruit around it moldy as well. Therefore, obscene talk involves any language that is rotten. This kind of language is not pleasant or kind, and it does not create anything good. Obscene talk only spreads sin.

So when it comes to our tongues, we should be careful about what we speak. But we should also understand the connection between our mouths and our hearts. Jesus teaches us in Luke 6:45 that our words reveal what is in our hearts. If our hearts are centered upon and focused on what is good and godly, our mouths will reflect our hearts. But if our hearts are centered upon and focused on what is unrighteous and ungodly, our speech will be rotten. What leaves our mouths reveals the condition of our hearts, and we should take this condition seriously.

From Death to Life

As believers, if obscene talk is part of our vocabulary, there may be a disconnect between what we confess to believe and how we are living. If we confess belief in Christ—the One who is perfect, beautiful, and holy—then our lives should reflect who Jesus is. This means our mouths should reflect who Christ is. If we confess belief in Christ, we have also received new, regenerated hearts. We have had our sinful hearts cleansed by Christ's blood. Therefore, if what leaves our mouths is rotten, we should consider what we are absorbing and focusing on that is keeping our words from reflecting the regenerated hearts we have been given in Christ.

Instead of speaking obscenely, Scripture tells us to "let your speech always be gracious, seasoned with salt, so that you may know how you should answer each person" (Colossians 4:6). Ephesians 4:29 instructs that we are to speak words that build up and give grace to others.

These verses teach us that our speech should be Christlike. Our words should reflect His words. And we are able to speak like Christ because we have been made new. The new selves we have been given through Christ enable us to speak graciously.

How would our words change if we daily thought, *How can I give grace to others by the way I speak? How can I build up others through my speech?* Having this mindset can greatly impact how we speak. But ultimately, being in God's Word is what will help us the most in this area. If our words reveal what is in our hearts, we must fill our hearts with the truth of God's Word. This begs the question, what are we consuming? Are we filling our hearts with what Scripture says and affirms? Or are we consuming media that is only fueling rottenness within?

> The new selves we have been given through Christ enable us to speak graciously.

When we prioritize God's Word and meditate on what Scripture says, the truth of God's Word will fill and remain in our hearts. And when our hearts are filled with the truth of God's Word, our mouths will reflect what is in our hearts. May our words be gracious in response to the truth and goodness of God's Word. May the words we speak point others to the One who has transformed our hearts and lives.

day thirty-four reflection

Read Ephesians 5:4. What makes thankfulness more suitable for followers of Christ than obscene and foolish talking?

How can you point others to Christ by the way you speak?

Spend some time in prayer, asking the Lord to reveal anything in your heart that is leading to rotten speech. Confess these things to the Lord and ask Him to fill your heart with what is pleasing to Him.

"May the words we speak point others to the One who has transformed our hearts and lives."

When I Survey the Wondrous Cross

Isaac Watts

1 When I sur-vey the won-drous cross on which the Prince of glo-ry died, my rich-est gain I count but loss, and pour con-tempt on all my pride.
2 For-bid it, Lord, that I should boast save in the death of Christ, my God! All the vain things that charm me most, I sac-ri-fice them through his blood.
3 See, from his head, his hands, his feet, sor-row and love flow min-gled down. Did e'er such love and sor-row meet, or thorns com-pose so rich a crown?
4 Were the whole realm of na-ture mine, that were a pres-ent far too small. Love so a-maz-ing, so di-vine, de-mands my soul, my life, my all.

Read Matthew 27:45–54.

Reflect on this hymn and how it encourages or challenges you.

--- Ways This Hymn Encourages Me ---

--- Ways This Hymn Challenges Me ---

part three

Hope for Our Sin

DAY THIRTY-FIVE

As believers, we have been brought from death to life, and this radical transformation impacts the way we live.

day thirty-five

LIVING OUT OUR FREEDOM

Read Romans 6:11–23

As we turn to part three of this study, it is possible that you feel a certain heaviness after spending twenty-four days diving into the sins we often struggle with as believers. Perhaps, as you journeyed through part two, you felt convicted of certain sins that your eyes were opened to, or perhaps you were reminded of specific sins that you have fought against for a while. Even though the gospel was woven throughout part two, it is easy to still feel a bit hopeless in light of the weight of our sin.

This is why part three will focus on the hope we have for our sin. As we begin to wrap up this study, we will take a look at the truths of Scripture that fuel our hope even as we struggle with sin. We will explore how Christ's forgiveness, sympathy, power, and victory can—and do—comfort and encourage us. And we will end by seeing how our eternal home in the future gives us hope in the present.

Before we dive into these topics, it is helpful for us to consider what it looks like to live out our freedom in Christ. We have talked a lot about Christ's grace, forgiveness, and mercy, and while we should look to Christ's grace daily, especially when we sin, we should not take Christ's grace for granted. We should not think that because we have Christ's forgiveness, we are free to do what we please.

As believers, we have been brought from death to life, and this radical transformation impacts the way we live. Because we are "dead to sin and alive to God in Christ Jesus" (Romans 6:11), we look at our sin and treat our sin differently than how we once did apart from Christ. Romans 6:12–14 shows us that as believers, we are to respond to our new life in Christ by rejecting our sin. Because we have been set free from our sin, we are to fight against our sin. And while this struggle is difficult, Paul reminds us in Romans 6:14 that sin does not rule over us because we are under grace.

Because Christ has saved us by His grace and set us free from sin, we are to obey Him willingly and joyfully. We are to not see God's grace as license to do what we please.

Instead, we are to respond to God's great grace with faithfulness and obedience.

So, as we move forward in this study, let us certainly marvel at the hope we have in Christ while also responding with obedience to the Lord. Yes, Jesus gives us His forgiveness, sympathy, victory, and more. But we should respond to those gifts with joyful submission and obedience to the Lord. "For freedom, Christ set us free" (Galatians 5:1), so let us live in light of our freedom in Christ by serving the Lord.

day thirty-five reflection

Write a prayer below, asking God to help you live in light of your freedom in Christ.

DAY THIRTY-SIX

Because Christ's forgiveness is freely given,
His constant grace remains secure
no matter our sins and struggles.

day thirty-six

REMEMBERING CHRIST'S FORGIVENESS

Read Ephesians 1:7–9, 1 John 1:9

The battle against sin can be fierce, and even though we may know we have freedom in Christ, we might struggle to believe that Christ has forgiven us. When we commit a certain sin that we have been trying to overcome, we can feel unforgivable. When the devil reminds us of a certain sin from our past, we can be overcome by guilt and shame.

On Day 27 of our study, we discussed how we can forgive others because Christ has forgiven us. While we are to remember the gospel when we struggle to forgive others, we are to also remember the gospel when we sin. It is only by resting in the gospel that we receive peace in light of our sin and are released from guilt and shame. As we will discuss below, the gospel reminds us that Christ's forgiveness is freely given, sufficient, and eternal.

Let us first discuss the concept that Christ's forgiveness is freely given. When Jesus went to the cross, He did not die for those with only certain qualities. He did not die for those who were better than others, for Scripture tells us that all people are sinners who have fallen short of the glory of God (Romans 3:23). It does not matter who we are or what we have done; there is nothing we need to do to receive Christ's forgiveness except turn to Him and repent of our sin. Jesus does not ask us to clean ourselves up in order for us to receive His forgiveness. He does not tell us to obey all of God's commands perfectly before we can have His forgiveness. Jesus gives us His forgiveness completely and freely.

Because Christ's forgiveness is freely given, we do not have to worry that we can somehow influence or change Christ's forgiveness. If Christ's forgiveness had certain conditions beyond our turning to Him and believing in Him, His forgiveness would be able to change based on our actions—His forgiveness would be dependent upon what we do. But because Christ's forgiveness is freely given, His constant grace remains secure no matter our sins and struggles. This is good news for us on the days when we feel like we keep messing up. Knowing that Christ continues to give us His forgiveness freely assures us that we will always remain forgiven.

Christ's forgiveness is also sufficient. This means that Christ's forgiveness covers all of our sins. Centuries before Christ came, God set up a system of sacrifice for His people, by which they could offer the blood of an unblemished animal to receive forgiveness for their sins. In fact, Hebrews 9:22b tells us that "without the shedding of blood there is no forgiveness." But these sacrifices had to be made over and over again. When Jesus came, however, He spilled His blood on the cross and died "once for all time" (Hebrews 9:12). Because Jesus Christ was the all-perfect, all-sufficient sacrifice, God's people no longer have to continually offer the blood of animals.

If Jesus's forgiveness only covered our sins in part, this would mean that Jesus's sacrifice was not sufficient. But when Jesus went to the cross, there was no deficiency in His sacrifice. Therefore, the forgiveness that Jesus made possible through His sacrifice on the cross is totally sufficient to cover all our sins. Because Jesus was the perfect sacrifice, He paid the debt we owe for our sin and satisfied God's wrath through His death, and we are completely forgiven. There was no flaw in God's plan of redemption through Christ.

Because Christ's forgiveness is sufficient, we do not have to fear that Christ's grace will only cover some of our sins. We do not have to worry that God will only forgive minor sins but will not forgive us for more serious sins. Christ's forgiveness covers all our sins—no matter how great or small. And because Christ's forgiveness is total, we do not have to fear punishment from God for our sins, though we can still experience earthly consequences. As we have already covered in this study, Romans 8:1 powerfully declares that there is "now no condemnation for those in Christ Jesus." If Jesus's forgiveness was ineffective, we would still have to be punished for our sins. But because of Christ's perfect sacrifice, we have confidence that there is no condemnation for our sin.

Lastly, we will discuss the truth that Jesus's forgiveness is eternal. Because His forgiveness is sufficient, it is also eternal. The author of Hebrews confirms this when he writes, "But this man [Jesus], after offering one sacrifice for sins forever, sat down at the right hand of God. He is now waiting until his enemies are made his footstool. For by one offering he has perfected forever those who are sanctified" (Hebrews 10:12–14). Jesus's perfect sacrifice ensures that His forgiveness will never run out. Because Jesus is God and because He accomplished all that our sin demanded on the cross, we have Christ's forgiveness always.

One way we know this to be true is because of what Scripture says about the Great White Throne. One day, all people—both believers and unbelievers—will stand before God's throne to be judged (Revelation 20:11–15). Those who do not know Christ will be sent away and separated from God forever. But those who do know Christ will be welcomed into eternal life. These Scriptures reveal how believers will stand forgiven when they go before the Great White Throne one day because of Christ. Therefore, if we know we will stand forgiven before God in the future, we can be assured that we remain forgiven in the present.

Christ's freely given, sufficient, and eternal forgiveness gives us peace and security when we sin. Knowing that God will be faithful to always forgive our sins encourages us to confidently come to God with our sins. Knowing that there is no condemnation for those of us in Christ assures us that when we go to the Lord, we will not be punished for our sins.

And knowing that Christ forgives all of our sins—past, present, and future—washes away our guilt and shame. So when we find ourselves discouraged by our sin or overwhelmed with shame, we can remember and rest in Christ and His forgiveness. The more we rest in Christ's forgiveness, the more peace we will experience as we wrestle with and fight against our sin.

> Knowing that Christ forgives all of our sins — past, present, and future — washes away our guilt and shame.

day thirty-six reflection

What do these aspects of Christ's forgiveness say about who Jesus is?

What aspect of Christ's forgiveness (freely given, sufficient, eternal) resonates with you the most and why?

What would it look like for you to rest in these truths of Christ's forgiveness when you sin?

DAY THIRTY-SEVEN

Jesus understands our weaknesses
and struggles with sin,
and He is with us in the fight.

day thirty-seven

DWELLING ON CHRIST'S SYMPATHY

Read Hebrews 4:14–16

Likely all of us have experienced a time when we felt alone. Perhaps we endured a season of grief and felt as if no one understood our pain. Or maybe we dealt with a difficult family circumstance and felt as if we were by ourselves in the struggle. We can all feel these feelings of loneliness, especially in our struggle against sin. Even though we know all believers wrestle with sin, it is possible for us to feel alone in the fight. Not only this but we may be tempted to believe that God does not know or care about our struggle with sin. Therefore, when we feel weighed down by our sin or tired from the fight, we can believe that we are utterly alone. But we are not alone. Jesus understands our weaknesses and struggles with sin, and He is with us in the fight.

How does Jesus know our weaknesses and struggles with sin? Because He experienced what it was like to be weak Himself. Jesus willingly came to earth as a human for us. While Jesus maintained His full divinity, He also assumed "the form of a servant, taking on the likeness of humanity" (Philippians 2:7). This means that Jesus became fully human. Becoming human, Jesus experienced what it was like to be tired, hungry, and thirsty. But Jesus also experienced what it was like to be tempted. The Gospel accounts reveal how Jesus was tempted in the wilderness by Satan (Matthew 4:1–11, Luke 4:1–13). However, Jesus did not give into Satan's temptation, but instead, He obeyed God perfectly.

As a human, Jesus likely experienced many other moments of temptation that were not recorded explicitly in Scripture. Even though we do not know of these instances, Hebrews 4:15 tells us that Jesus was tempted "in every way as we are, yet without sin." Though Jesus faced temptation and weakness, He never gave in to sin and temptation. Because Jesus never sinned, He was able to be our perfect sacrifice. Romans 8:3 declares,

"For what the law could not do since it was weakened by the flesh, God did. He condemned sin in the flesh by sending his own Son in the likeness of sinful flesh as a sin offering." Through His perfect obedience, Jesus fulfilled the righteous requirement of the Law. On the cross, Jesus gave us His perfect righteousness in place of our unrighteousness, securing our salvation.

Because of Christ's perfect humanity, we are able to be forgiven. But because of Christ's perfect humanity, we are also able to be understood. Jesus knows exactly what it is like to experience temptation because He experienced temptation Himself. Therefore, Jesus knows how we feel when we struggle with temptation. He sympathizes with us in our weaknesses; it is as if He whispers to us, *I know what you are going through.*

> The kindness and understanding of our Savior move us toward Him when we are in need of His help.

The truth that Jesus knows and understands our weaknesses and struggles with sin comforts us. When temptation looms large, we do not have to feel as if we are all alone. We have a Savior who is with us in the fight against sin and sympathizes with us in the fight. Because Jesus understands our struggles and sympathizes with us, we are encouraged to go to Him. We do not serve a God who is cold or indifferent to us when we wrestle with our sin. We serve a God who wraps us in a warm embrace and reminds us that He understands. Hebrews 4:16 instructs us that in light of Christ's sympathy, we are to "approach the throne of grace with boldness, so that we may receive mercy and find grace to help us in time of need." The kindness and understanding of our Savior move us toward Him when we are in need of His help.

Because Jesus faced every kind of temptation but did not sin, we are empowered to not give into temptation, which we will discuss more tomorrow. For now, we can find comfort in remembering that Jesus understands our struggle against temptation, and we can also be comforted by the reminder that Jesus has triumphed over temptation. If we are in Christ, we are able to be like our Savior through our obedience. With the power of the Holy Spirit in us, we are empowered to triumph in the face of temptation and choose obedience to God instead.

So, when we feel alone in our struggle against sin, let us remember that Christ is with us. When we feel overwhelmed and discouraged, let us remember that Christ understands. And when we feel too weak to keep fighting, let us remember that Christ empowers us. As believers, we have a faithful and sympathetic Savior who cares for us and understands us like no one else can.

day thirty-seven reflection

In what ways do you feel as if Christ does not understand your struggle against sin?

How does it encourage you to know that Christ understands your struggle and sympathizes with you?

How does the knowledge that Christ understands and sympathizes with you impact your fight against sin?

> We have a faithful and sympathetic Savior who cares for us and understands us like no one else can.

DAY THIRTY-EIGHT

Because of God's strength,
we are empowered and
equipped to battle our sin.

day thirty-eight

RESTING IN GOD'S POWER

Read Ephesians 3:20, Philippians 1:6

Have you ever gone on a hike and reached a point when you felt like you could not take another step? Or have you gone for a run or begun a workout and then felt too weak to continue? We are all limited as humans. We are not omnipotent, or all-powerful, like God is. Each one of us experiences weakness and tires at some point. However, we often act as if we do have limitless power. We try to do everything in our own strength, including fighting our sin. But trying to fight against sin in our own power is like trying to defeat a fierce monster without using the weapon we need to fight it. Our fight against sin is not a battle that we fight in our own strength. Because of God's strength, we are empowered and equipped to battle our sin.

We may know this to be true, but we can still try to fight against our sin in our own power. Doing so can lead to three consequences. The first consequence is that it causes us to become self-righteous and prideful. We might see the ways in which we are rejecting sin but then believe that success is due to our efforts alone. When others encourage us in the ways in which we have grown as a believer, we might think to ourselves, *That is all because of me and what I have done.*

The second consequence is that we can end up giving in to temptation rather than resisting it. This is because we are not strong enough to fight against temptation in our own power. And if we do not turn to God and ask for His help, we may find ourselves easily giving into temptation.

The third consequence is that we can become defeated and discouraged by our sins and struggles. Because we are too weak to fight against sin in our own power, we can feel beaten down and overwhelmed when we do not see ourselves successfully overcoming sin.

These three consequences remind us how God is the One who empowers us to fight sin, and He deserves all the glory for doing so (Ephesians 3:20). If we are in Christ, we have the power of God in us always. Through Christ's forgiveness and grace, we receive the Holy Spirit, who dwells within us and gives us permanent access to God's strength and power. Scripture tells us that God's divine power gives us all we need for life and godliness (2 Peter 1:3). This means that God's power gives us what we need to fight against our sin.

We also know this to be true because of what Paul says about the armor of God. In Ephesians 6:10–17, Paul describes the different elements that we should take up or embrace, such as prayer and truth, to battle well against spiritual darkness. The fact that Paul establishes this armor as the "armor of God" is enough to show us that God equips us with His power to fight against sin. But before Paul goes into detail about the armor of God, he instructs believers in verse 10 to be "strengthened by the Lord and by his vast strength." This verse reminds us that God's vast strength is what we need if we want to successfully fight against our own personal sin and the spiritual darkness around us. God has given this strength to us; we simply need to rely on Him.

God's Word also teaches us that God empowers us to escape temptation. We discussed earlier how we can easily give in to temptation when we try to fight our temptation in our own strength. But

> God is the One who empowers us to fight sin, and He deserves all the glory for doing so.

1 Corinthians 10:13 declares that God not only keeps us from being tempted beyond what we can handle, but He also provides us a way out of our temptation. Such truth should encourage us in the moments when temptation feels fierce. Rather than trying to resist temptation with our own strength, we can remember how God provides us a way out, and we can rely on His strength to do so.

Another amazing truth about God's power in us is that God's power will complete our sanctification (Philippians 1:6). As believers, we are all undergoing the process of sanctification, our becoming more like Christ. A major aspect of our sanctification involves choosing to walk in obedience instead of delighting in our sin. We cannot turn away from our sin and walk in obedience without God's strength (1 Thessalonians 5:23–24). Because God empowers us, He is the One who carries out our sanctification. And He is the One who will complete our sanctification. God started His good work of sanctification in us and will see that work through one day. While we await the day when Christ returns and our sanctification will be complete, we are able to have joy in our current sanctification. We are able to hope in the Lord as He sanctifies us. Not only is God carrying out our sanctification in the present, but He will complete our sanctification in the future, and that encourages us in our battle against sin.

So let us rely on God's power when it comes to fighting our sin rather than relying on our own. Each day, we can ask God to strengthen us in the battle against our flesh and to empower us in the moments when temptation is heavy. Whenever we see progress in our sanctification, let us be sure to give God all the glory for that progress. In the moments when we feel defeated by our sin or too weak in the battle against our flesh, may we rest in God's great power. And when we feel as if our fight against sin will never end, let us hope in the Lord and what He will do for us one day. God has gifted us His power by His grace, so may we rest in and rely on His strength as we fight.

> God's power gives us what we need to fight against our sin.

day thirty-eight reflection

In what ways do you rely on your own strength
when it comes to fighting sin?

Why do we need God's power to fight sin?

How can you practically rely on and rest in God's power?

DAY THIRTY-NINE

Our sin does not and cannot overcome or defeat us, for we are more than conquerors in Christ.

day thirty-nine

CELEBRATING CHRIST'S VICTORY

Read 1 Corinthians 15:50–58

Yesterday we talked about how God gives us His power to fight sin and that by God's power, our sanctification will be complete. This truth connects to another truth that gives us hope as we struggle with sin. Because of Christ, we have victory over our sin. Not only this, but one day, we will experience the fullness of that victory when Christ returns.

When Jesus died on the cross, it seemed as if all hope was lost. Jesus's disciples watched as the One who raised people from the dead breathed His last. These men thought that Jesus was going to change everything. After all, Jesus revealed to them that He was the Messiah, the Son of God (Matthew 16:13–20). Yet He died. While the disciples grieved the loss of their teacher, God's plan of redemption was unfolding. And three days after Christ's death, Jesus rose from the grave. When His disciples saw Him face to face, hope swelled up within them once again.

Jesus's death and resurrection declare Christ's victory over sin and death. Paul tells us in Colossians 2:14–15 that Jesus erased the debt we owe for our sin and nailed it to the cross. He also "disarmed the rulers and authorities" and "triumphed over them." These rulers and authorities are demonic powers—agents of darkness. Jesus triumphed over these powers by taking on the price of our sin and rising from the grave, demonstrating His power over sin and death. Jesus's death and resurrection show us that Jesus has won the victory. Sin and death do not have the ultimate power or final word—Jesus does. And those of us in Christ share in this victory.

Romans 8:37 powerfully declares that "we are more than conquerors through him who loved us." Because of Christ, those who trust and believe in Him take part in His triumphant victory. If we are in Christ, Jesus has broken the chains of our bondage to sin. He has removed the punishment we owe for our sin. And He has given us eternal life in Him. As followers of Christ, we are triumphant over sin and death because of Christ's sacrifice and salvation. This does not mean that we will not struggle with sin, as we have discussed. Rather, it means that our sin does not and cannot overcome or defeat us, for we are more than conquerors in Christ.

Christ's death and resurrection give us victory in the present. If we are in Christ, we can look at the sin we wrestle against with triumph rather than defeat. Fighting sin in the present is like fighting a war that has already been won. Being in a battle in which the other side is sure to lose causes one to fight even more boldly and victoriously. In the same way, because the battle has already been won, we are able to fight our sin with confidence.

> Jesus Christ is our great victor who will one day defeat sin and death once and for all.

Christ's death and resurrection also have eternal implications. First Corinthians 15:50–58 explains that when Christ returns, He will defeat sin and death once and for all. Death will be finally swallowed up forever, which means sin will be swallowed up forever. When this time comes, we will experience the fullness of Christ's victory because sin and death will be vanquished. We will also experience what it is like to have glorified bodies, permanently rid of sin. Paul makes it known that Jesus is the One who receives all the credit for this victory (1 Corinthians 15:57). Jesus Christ is our great victor who will one day defeat sin and death once and for all.

We sing a song of victory as followers of Christ. We sing this song in the present as we look to the cross and grave with joy and triumph. But we will sing this song with even more delight in the future when we will witness Christ's final defeat over sin and death. Therefore, the Christian life is a life of victory. Though the battle against sin can be fierce and long, it is not a battle we fight without hope. Christ has won the victory, and this truth changes how we view sin and death as believers. This truth reminds us that our sin cannot overpower us if we are in Christ. Our sin cannot overcome us because it has already been overcome on the cross. Knowing this gives us hope and confidence on the days when we feel discouraged about our sin. And knowing this gives us the motivation we need to keep fighting our sin with the help of the Holy Spirit.

As followers of Christ, may the cross and grave remind us that the battle has already been won. Though we still wage war against our sinful flesh, let us do so with triumph rather than defeat. And whenever we feel as if this battle will never end, let us look to Christ's promised return when He will vanquish sin and death forever.

day thirty-nine reflection

Are you currently operating with an attitude of victory or defeat when it comes to your sin? Why?

How does Christ's victory encourage you as you wrestle with sin?

How does the truth of Christ's victory impact those who do not know Christ? How might you share this aspect of the gospel with someone who is not a believer?

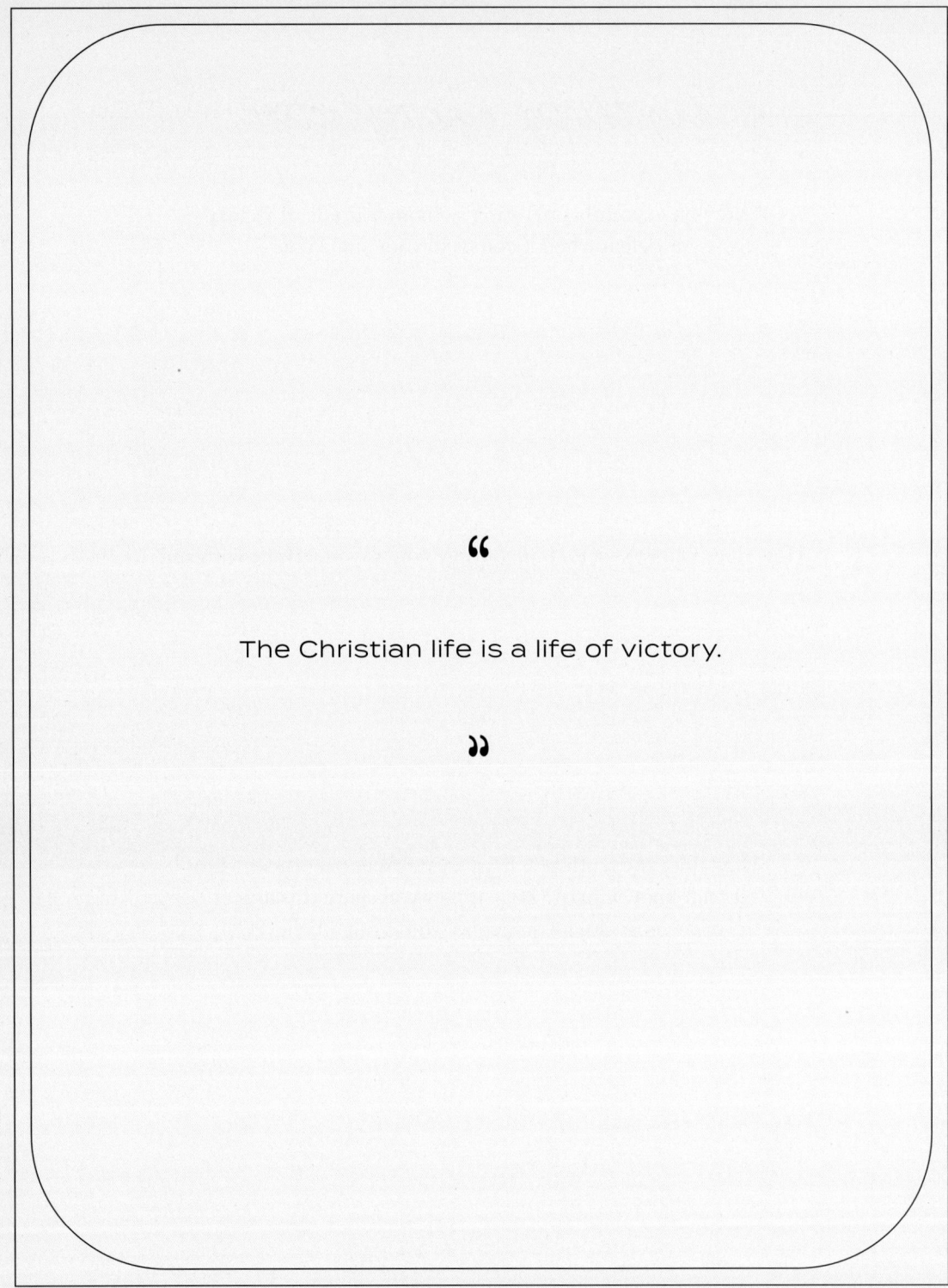

"The Christian life is a life of victory."

DAY FORTY

Our eternity with the Lord will be full of everlasting life and joy.

Day 40: Looking toward the Hope of Heaven

day forty

LOOKING TOWARD THE HOPE OF HEAVEN

Read Revelation 21

Imagine that you are in a battle that feels hard and heavy. The weather is overcast and gloomy, and just as you defeat some of the enemy's army, more come on the scene. But then suddenly, the sun breaks through the clouds and illuminates everything. Little by little, you watch as all the darkness around you starts to fade. The opposing army drops their weapons and falls to the ground, defeated. Every sad and evil thing in the world begins to vanish. You hear a triumphant song begin to play, and people's voices rise in praise as the King you have been fighting for comes into view.

This is a picture of what we will all experience as believers when Christ returns. Yesterday we talked about how we have victory in Christ and how the battle has already been won. When Christ returns, we will see the fullness of that victory, not just as sin is defeated but as God makes everything new. Revelation 21 shows us this reality and the hope of heaven for all those who trust and believe in Jesus. Within this chapter, we see three descriptions of heaven that bring great hope to those of us in Christ.

First, heaven is described as a place where God will dwell with His people. Verse 3 declares, "Look, God's dwelling is with humanity, and he will live with them. They will be his peoples, and God himself will be with them and will be their God." Such truth reveals how there will be no separation between us and God. While there is a degree of separation between us and God in the present, there will be no separation in the future. God's full presence will come to dwell with His people. This dwelling between us and God will be permanent. Nothing will threaten our relationship with Him. Nothing will cause us to be separated from Him. As believers, we will be with God, and He will be with us forever.

Second, heaven is described as a place where there will be no more sin and suffering. Verse 4 tells us that God will wipe the tears from our eyes and that death, grief, crying, and pain will be no more. Why? "Because the previous things have passed away." These "previous things" include all that is sinful, evil, and corruptible in the world. With sin fully defeated and removed, there will be nothing to hurt us or bring us pain. All that grieves and overwhelms us today will be gone forever. We will never experience suffering again, nor will we deal with the heaviness of death. Our eternity with the Lord will be full of everlasting life and joy.

Finally, heaven is described as a place where everything will be made new. God promises this truth in verse 5. This hope connects with the first two descriptions of heaven that we discussed. Because God is making all things new, we will dwell with Him fully and experience a world without sin and suffering. God will restore all that is broken and establish an earth that is perfect. This means that we, too, will receive full restoration. The world will be made new, and we will be made new along with it. All believers will receive new, glorified bodies that will be without sin.

Revelation 21:7 tells us that the hope of heaven is given to those who conquer. As we saw yesterday, if we are in Christ, we are more than conquerors (Romans 8:37). Therefore, the hope of heaven will be given to all believers. Christ's grace will preserve us as we live here in the present and will carry us into the future, where we will dwell with Him eternally. But what does this mean for us now? How do the promises of eternity affect us in the present?

First, these promises give us assurance that we will one day experience what it is like to live without sin. In eternity, we will not struggle with sin personally or witness the destruction sin causes around us. This truth encourages us in our current struggle with sin. Even though wrestling with sin is hard, we can be cheered, knowing that this struggle will come to an end. One day we will never again battle against sin. One day we will never again experience temptation. Because God will make all things new in the future, we can have peace in the present, even though sin remains currently.

> Because God will make all things new in the future, we can have peace in the present.

Second, these promises help us persevere. Knowing that we will not remain in a sinful world encourages us to press on in our obedience and faithfulness to God. If our future was bleak and without hope, we would likely want to give up. We would probably wonder about the point of fighting our sin and being faithful to God if there was no hope in the end. But because we know the hope of heaven, we are able to persevere on this side of eternity. We are able to boldly and joyfully slay our sin with confidence. Because God will make all things new in the future, we can endure the fight against sin in the present.

While it is difficult to live on this side of eternity, the hope of heaven comforts us. It reminds us how this struggle against sin is only temporary, and one day, we will live without the presence of sin. So even though the weight of sin still presses down upon us, we are able to push back with the strength of the Spirit. We are able to persevere and keep fighting with God's strength. May the hope of heaven fill us with peace and encourage us to draw near to the One who gives us this hope. Because of Jesus, we have an everlasting hope, a living hope (1 Peter 1:3). Let us lift our voices in worship and praise our great King who secures our salvation, gives us an eternal home, and brings us from death to life.

> Because we know the hope of heaven, we are able to persevere on this side of eternity.

day forty reflection

Of the three descriptions of heaven that we discussed in this study day (that God will be with His people forever, that there will be no more sin and suffering, and that everything will be made new), which resonates most with you?

In what ways can you rest in the hope of heaven when you struggle with sin?

Spend some time in prayer, thanking Christ for securing this hope of heaven for you and asking Him to keep you focused on this hope.

Christ the Lord is Risen Today

Charles Wesley

1. Christ the Lord is risen to-day,— Al - le - lu - ia! Earth and heaven in cho-rus say,— Al - le - lu - ia! Raise your joys and tri-umphs high, Al - le - lu - ia! Sing,— ye— heavens, and earth re - ply,— Al - le - lu - ia!
2. Love's re-deem-ing work is done,— Al - le - lu - ia! Fought the fight, the bat - tle won, Al - le - lu - ia! Death in vain for-bids him rise, Al - le - lu - ia! Christ— has o - pened pa - ra - dise, Al - le - lu - ia!
3. Lives a-gain our glo-rious King, Al - le - lu - ia! Where, O death, is now thy sting? Al - le - lu - ia! Once he died our souls to save, Al - le - lu - ia! Where's thy vic-to-ry, boas-ting grave? Al - le - lu - ia!
4. Soar we now where Christ has led,— Al - le - lu - ia! Fol-lowing our ex-al-ted Head, Al - le - lu - ia! Made like him, like him we rise, Al - le - lu - ia! Ours— the cross, the grave, the skies,— Al - le - lu - ia!
5. Hail the Lord of earth and heaven, Al - le - lu - ia! Praise to thee by both be given, Al - le - lu - ia! Thee we greet tri-um-phant now, Al - le - lu - ia! Hail the Re - sur - rec - tion, thou,— Al - le - lu - ia!
6. King of glo-ry, soul of bliss,— Al - le - lu - ia! E - ver - las-ting life is this, Al - le - lu - ia! Thee to know, thy power to prove, Al - le - lu - ia! Thus to sing, and thus to love,— Al - le - lu - ia!

Read John 20:1–18.

Reflect on this hymn and how it encourages or challenges you.

— Ways This Hymn Encourages Me —

— Ways This Hymn Challenges Me —

"
We are to respond to
God's great grace with
faithfulness and obedience.
"

What is *the* Gospel?

Thank you for reading and enjoying this study with us! We are abundantly grateful for the Word of God, the instruction we glean from it, and the ever-growing understanding it provides for us of God's character. We are also thankful that Scripture continually points to one thing in innumerable ways: the gospel.

We remember our brokenness when we read about the fall of Adam and Eve in the garden of Eden (Genesis 3), where sin entered into a perfect world and maimed it. We remember the necessity that something innocent must die to pay for our sin when we read about the atoning sacrifices in the Old Testament. We read that we have all sinned and fallen short of the glory of God (Romans 3:23) and that the penalty for our brokenness, the wages of our sin, is death (Romans 6:23). We all need grace and mercy, but most importantly, we all need a Savior.

We consider the goodness of God when we realize that He did not plan to leave us in this dire state. We see His promise to buy us back from the clutches of sin and death in Genesis 3:15. And we see that promise accomplished with Jesus Christ on the cross. Jesus Christ knew no sin yet became sin so that we might become righteous through His sacrifice (2 Corinthians 5:21). Jesus was tempted in every way that we are and lived sinlessly. He was reviled yet still yielded Himself for our sake, that we may have life abundant in Him. Jesus lived the perfect life that we could not live and died the death that we deserved.

The gospel is profound yet simple. There are many mysteries in it that we will never understand this side of heaven, but there is still overwhelming weight to its implications in this life. The gospel tells of our sinfulness and God's goodness and a gracious gift that compels a response. We are saved by grace through faith, which means that we rest with faith in the grace that Jesus Christ displayed on the cross (Ephesians 2:8–9). We cannot save ourselves from our brokenness or do any amount of good works to merit God's favor. Still, we can have faith that what Jesus accomplished in His death, burial, and resurrection was more than enough for our salvation and our eternal delight. When we accept God, we are commanded to die to ourselves and our sinful desires and live a life worthy of the calling we have received (Ephesians 4:1). The gospel compels us to be sanctified, and in so doing, we are conformed to the likeness of Christ Himself. This is hope. This is redemption. This is the gospel.

Scriptures to Reference

GENESIS 3:15

I will put hostility between you and the woman, and between your offspring and her offspring. He will strike your head, and you will strike his heel.

ROMANS 3:23

For all have sinned and fall short of the glory of God.

ROMANS 6:23

For the wages of sin is death, but the gift of God is eternal life in Christ Jesus our Lord.

2 CORINTHIANS 5:21

He made the one who did not know sin to be sin for us, so that in him we might become the righteousness of God.

EPHESIANS 2:8-9

For you are saved by grace through faith, and this is not from yourselves; it is God's gift—not from works, so that no one can boast.

EPHESIANS 4:1-3

Therefore I, the prisoner in the Lord, urge you to walk worthy of the calling you have received, with all humility and gentleness, with patience, bearing with one another in love, making every effort to keep the unity of the Spirit through the bond of peace.

BIBLIOGRAPHY

Barclay, William. *The Gospel of Matthew*. 3rd ed. The New Daily Study Bible. Edinburgh: Saint Andrew Press, 2001.

Cole, R. Alan. *Exodus: An Introduction and Commentary*. Vol. 2 of Tyndale Old Testament Commentaries. Downers Grove, IL: InterVarsity Press, 1973.

Cole, R. Alan. *Galatians: An Introduction and Commentary*. Vol. 9 of Tyndale New Testament Commentaries. Downers Grove, IL: InterVarsity Press, 1989.

Cole, R. Alan. *Mark: An Introduction and Commentary*. Vol. 2 of Tyndale New Testament Commentaries. Downers Grove, IL: InterVarsity Press, 1989.

Commentary. Grand Rapids, MI: William B. Eerdmans Publishing Company, 2008.

DeYoung, Kevin. "15 Ways to Fight Lust with the Sword of the Spirit." *The Gospel Coalition*. August, 26, 2015. https://www.thegospelcoalition.org/blogs/kevin-deyoung/15-ways-to-fight-lust-with-the-sword-of-the-spirit/.

DeYoung, Kevin. "What is Hypocrisy?" *The Gospel Coalition*. December 13, 2012. https://www.thegospelcoalition.org/blogs/kevin-deyoung/what-is-hypocrisy/.

Foulkes, Francis. *Ephesians: An Introduction and Commentary*. Vol. 10 of Tyndale New Testament Commentaries. Downers Grove, IL: InterVarsity Press, 1989.

Grudem, Wayne A. *1 Peter: An Introduction and Commentary*. Vol. 17 of Tyndale New Testament Commentaries. Downers Grove, IL: InterVarsity Press, 1988.

Hart, Joseph. "Come, Ye Sinners, Poor and Needy." 1759. *Hymnary.org*. https://hymnary.org/text/come_ye_sinners_poor_and_needy_weak_and.

Hubbard, Scott. "Do Everything Without Grumbling." *Desiring God*. May 10, 2019. https://www.desiringgod.org/articles/do-everything-without-grumbling.

Lowry, Robert. "Nothing But the Blood of Jesus." 1876. *Hymnary.org*. https://hymnary.org/text/what_can_wash_away_my_sin.

Mitchell, Matt. "What Is Gossip? Exposing a Common and Dangerous Sin." *Desiring God*. May 26, 2021. https://www.desiringgod.org/articles/what-is-gossip.

Moo, Douglas J. *The Letter of James*. The Pillar New Testament Commentary. Grand Rapids, MI: William B. Eerdmans Publishing Company, 2000.